out

of the

ordinary

Books by Joyce Rupp:

Fresh Bread

Praying Our Goodbyes

May I Have This Dance?

The Cup of Our Life

May I Walk You Home?

(Ave Maria Press)

Dear Heart Come Home

Your Sorrow Is My Sorrow

(Crossroad Publishing Company)

The Star in My Heart

Prayers to Sophia

(Innisfree Press)

Little Pieces of Light

(Paulist Press)

Cassette Tapes

All of Life Is a Holy Festival

Befriend the Darkness, Welcome the Light

Meeting God in Our Transition Times

Walking With Those Who Hurt

(Ave Maria Press)

Videos

Spiritual Growth in Tough Times (set of 3)

(Corpus Video)

out

of the

ordinary

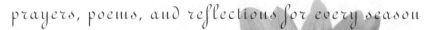
prayers, poems, and reflections for every season

Joyce

Rupp

ave maria press   Notre Dame, Indiana

First printing, December 1999

Third printing, January 2002

60,000 copies in print

International Standard Book Number: 0-87793-920-9

Cover and text design by K. H. Coney

Printed and bound in the United States of America.

Library of Congress Cataloging-in-Publication Data

Rupp, Joyce.
      Out of the ordinary : prayers, poems, and reflections for every season / Joyce Rupp.
            p. cm.
ISBN 087793-920-9 (pbk.)
1. Worship programs. 2. Church year. I. Title.

BV198 .R84 2000
242'.3--dc21   99-052395

I gratefully dedicate this book
of resources to:

all who prayed these prayers
with me in retreats and conferences,

all who have been welcoming recipients
of my seasonal reflections,

all who encourage me to write
and who love me into fuller life.

Acknowledgments

Each time I complete a manuscript I sit back and sigh with both satisfaction and relief. As I do so, I am keenly aware that the words on the pages are not just my own. They come from many sources of support and inspiration. More and more I see myself as a "gatherer" who gleans from the "spiritual fields" of many beautiful women and men whom I have met. As I look back on the shaping and writing of *Out of the Ordinary* there are particular persons to whom I owe much gratitude:

—Courtney Ramsay, who participated in a retreat that I facilitated in Grand Coteau, Louisiana, and who suggested the title for this book.

—Carola Broderick and Ginny Silvestri, who spent many hours reading my first draft and gave me their skillful, insightful opinions and suggestions for revising and adapting the text.

—Rev. Art McCann who helped me significantly with his life experience and practical suggestions.

—Janet Barnes, Dorothy Sullivan, Bernice Lightbourn, Dorothy Clemens, and the many others who have affirmed me by the prayerful quality of their lives and their daily intention of prayer for my ministry.

—Bernice Donovan who sent me the DeGrazia postcard with the print of the Fourteenth Station. This inspired an Easter reflection.

—Kathleen O'Daniel who graciously allowed me time and space in her country home, a retreat place filled with the kindness and love of her presence.

—Linda Hess, Bridget Pasker, and Joe Koelling, who brought the chants in the Appendix to life on CD and tape.

—Bob Hamma from Ave Maria Press, whose editorial expertise is always a gift to me.

—Sandra Bury, Pat Skinner, and Mary Kunkel who gift me with renewed dedication and vitality each Wednesday morning when we meet at dawn for our weekly ritual.

—Pastor and good friend, Tom Pfeffer, and the congregation of Visitation Parish who welcome me for chant and meditation on the scriptures.

—And all those who stand so faithfully with me and cheer me on: my mother, my siblings, my Servite community, and all my treasured friends.

Contents

Introduction

In my early years of ministry as a spiritual director and retreat leader, it seemed like I was always searching for an appropriate prayer or ritual to use with individuals or groups. It was difficult to find many resources that appealed to me or that were adequate for the situation. Eventually, I started writing my own prayers and rituals to fit what was needed. I began doing this at least fifteen years ago, so my files have gotten fatter and fatter with all these rituals and prayers that I have stuffed into them.

During those years I also developed a pattern of sending reflections on various liturgical and seasonal celebrations to my family and friends when I corresponded with them. These included some of my favorite celebrations such as Thanksgiving and Valentine's Day. Writing and sending the poems and reflections was a great way for me to enter more deeply into each of those occasions because I began listening inside and outside of myself long before the day arrived. This practice helped me enter into the heart of those celebrations in a much more focused and meaningful way.

It occurred to me some time ago that I might publish the prayers, rituals, poems, and reflections rather than have them remain unused in my files. I wanted others to have these resources available for their use. It was with this in mind that I gathered together many of the following resources and edited them for this book.

The Ordinariness of Life

I struggled with a title for this resource book until the weekend I was facilitating a retreat with a marvelous group of women in Grand Coteau, Louisiana. As we sat around the dinner table that evening I described the type of prayers and rituals that were in the book and asked them to think of a title for it. It wasn't long before Courtney said, "*Out of the Ordinary!*" I was astounded at how she had caught the flavor of these resources because she was right on target. Each selection does come out of the *ordinary*. I simply cannot imagine a prayer, poem, or reflection not being connected with the commonness of life, for it is there that I experience who I am and how God is with me. The resources in this book reflect my process of connecting this ordinariness of life with the extra-ordinariness of God.

Thus, as I seek to relate to God through prayer, I do not step out of the reality of my life. Rather, I step into it more fully with a keen sense that this is where my spiritual transformation occurs. Whenever I create a ritual or prayer I am constantly finding symbols and metaphors from my physical surroundings, from my mental and emotional world, and from the events and experiences that are part of my life as a human being. One of my favorite poets, Jane Kenyon, was fond of quoting Ezra Pound, who said, "The natural object is always the adequate symbol." It is the natural objects of my life that often spark my spiritual awareness and provide me with metaphors for the prayers I create. I hope that these metaphors will bring inspiration and meaning to you as well.

The other dimension of the suggested title that caught my attention was how these prayers are probably not the ordinary ones we would normally use. By offering them, I hope to re-energize our relationship with the divine, to keep it vibrant and alive through the imagery and various approaches I have suggested. My goal is to revitalize the spiritual blood pulsing through the veins of faith. Creative approaches to prayer can catch our attention and draw us to deeper levels of spiritual growth. Moving out of some of the regular ways that we pray can help us to breathe new life into our relationship with the Holy One. I hope this happens as these resources are used.

All of the resources contained in *Out of the Ordinary* are grounded on my firm belief in the indwelling presence of God. In the past, I was programmed theologically to focus on the transcendent God (almighty, everlasting, omnipotent, above and beyond). This approach of transcendence has not been adequate for me in establishing a relationship with the Divine Companion who breathes within my breath. It is in the relationship of the Holy One's "nearness" that I find consolation, inspiration, challenge, and a desire for sturdier commitment. It is this quality of immanence that has helped me to develop greater intimacy with the divine.

Using This Book of Resources

Our own approach and metaphors are the best for our personal prayer, but sometimes we need the yeast of someone else's prayer to get our own started. Any of the pages of this book can be used for personal prayer and reflection. Some were created specifically with the individual in mind (e.g., "A Birthday Reflection," "A Ritual for Aging," "Searching for Oneself," etc.). I hope that these reflections will serve as catalysts for personal reflection and that they will aid in deepening your own insights and awareness of the various feasts and celebrations.

These resources can also be used for communal gatherings. In fact, many of the rituals are oriented toward that purpose. When we pray communally, we often need common words to thread our spirits together as we attempt to join our hearts in union with the Holy One. The poems, prayers, and reflections can be used for small groups or for congregational worship. They could also be beneficial as homily starters and for planning retreat themes or days of renewal.

Some of the resources stand alone as rituals complete in themselves (e.g., "Light Our Way," "Remembering Our Spiritual Ancestors," "Blessing of One Who Draws Near to Death"). Some prayers could be used as sections of a much larger ritual that you would develop (e.g., "Magnificat to the God of Dawn," "Catechist's Prayer," "A Springtime Prayer"). Others are prayers that you might want to use as an alternative reading for a liturgy or a parish gathering. The decision is yours.

As for the topics and themes of these resources, they are many, but probably not as many as you would want. You will find some celebrations and aspects of life totally missing (e.g., wedding anniversaries, Memorial Day). You will find more selections under some topic areas than in others (e.g., "Difficult Times" has a lot because this is often a related theme for the retreats I give; "Easter" also has many selections because I like this feast very much). However, if there are only a few selections (or no selections) it does not indicate an aversion on my part. It may mean that some of my prayers and reflections were used in other publications of mine or that I simply have not created anything new on that particular theme.

These resources are offered humbly, knowing how unique each of us is and how impossible it is to create a prayer or ritual that could possibly meet everyone's needs. My language in relating to the Holy One and my naming of divinity may be different from what you want or need. You may desire to change the style or format of a ritual for

out of the ordinary

yourself, for congregational needs, for limitations of physical space, greater clarity, or other reasons. Use the rituals and prayers as seeds or as whole plants. Either way is fine with me. *I do ask, however, that the poems remain as they are. Any change of wording of the poems would require permission to do so.*

The Chants

As I have led rituals and prayer experiences I have found the use of chant to be extremely helpful. The repetition of words and melodies in chant helps to center and calm the human mind and heart. For a chant to be helpful in this manner, it needs to be sung for at least three minutes. However, sometimes it is appropriate and helpful to use a chant as a repetitive response throughout a ritual where it is sung only once or twice each time. The chants that I have created are in the Appendix. They are available on cassette and CD from Ave Maria Press and are entitled *Out of the Ordinary: Chants*. You may have favorite chants of your own or songs that would be more appropriate within the context of certain prayers and rituals in this book.

Permission Is Not Needed But Acknowledgment Is

Ave Maria Press has graciously honored my request that the resources in this book may be copied for personal and liturgical use without requiring permission from the publishing company. It is imperative, however, that you give adequate acknowledgment to the source of the prayer, poem, or reflection that you are copying. Much published work is "lost" because of carelessness or hurriedness when the source is not given on a printed page of material. Each page that you copy from this book must include the copyright acknowledgment text printed on the copyright page (page 4) of this book. Thank you for being attentive to this essential, necessary action.

Advent

The Present of Presence

God sent a present into the world, the gift of a loving presence named Jesus. The gospel stories indicate that Jesus gave few material things to people. What he gave most was his personal presence, gifts that were treasures of the heart: belief in self, inner healing, peace of mind, compassion, forgiveness, dignity, and justice. This loving presence lives on in us and is the central focus of Christmas gift-giving.

Sharing the gift of personal presence means that we see ourselves as a gift holding the goodness of Jesus who is Emmanuel, God-with-us. Like Jesus, we can give from our inner abundance, gifts from the heart. Moments lovingly spent with another through prayer or through personal presence carry more beauty and have more endurance than anything material we could give. What greater gifts could we share than ones that reflect the one Great Love we have known in the person of Jesus: our care and concern, our hope, our joy, our understanding and forgiveness, our kindness, our patience?

When I think of my hurried pace of life, I see myself as deeply entrenched in my western culture. I look at how Advent gets lost in "the Christmas rush." The messages are all around me: "Buy this and you will be happy; buy that and you will prove your love." Sharing presence is hard to do in a culture that keeps promoting material things as a sign of how much we love others. Sharing presence is difficult in an environment that encourages us to be as busy as possible so that we will be rich, successful, and important—and able to buy more things.

When we are busy, rushed, and pressed it is easy to miss awareness and union with those around us and with those in our larger world. Advent is a good season to be more deliberate in sharing the present of our presence every day. It may be through a phone call, a letter, a visit, or through the bonding of prayer as we focus love and attention toward those who need the strength of God to be with them.

The following are suggestions for "being with" others during Advent, one for each of the twenty-five days before Christmas. You may think of other ways to share your presence in order to deliberately choose "being" over "doing." When the feast of Christmas arrives

out of the ordinary

may you be more aware of the power of Emmanuel's presence within you and your ability to warm the lives of others because of this Gift of Love.

Suggestions for Giving the Present of Presence

Here are two possible ways to be with someone: (a) be physically present with another or (b) be present "in spirit" by deliberately sending prayer, compassionate thoughts, and kind feelings toward another person or group. Either approach could be appropriate for each of the following suggestions.

Be with someone who needs you.

Be with a person who gives you hope.

Be with those who live in terror and fear.

Be with an older person.

Be with someone who has helped you to grow.

Be with one who is in pain.

Be with a war-torn country.

Be with yourself.

Be with someone who has written to you.

Be with a child.

Be with a refugee who is fleeing from harm.

Be with an enemy or someone you dislike.

Be with a farmer losing his or her land.

Be with someone who has terminal illness.

Be with the homeless.

Be with those who suffer from substance abuse.

Be with hungry children.

Be with a coworker.

Be with those whose hope is faint.

Be with world leaders.

Be with someone in your family.

Be with men and women in prison.

Be with someone working for justice.

Be with those who are abused and neglected.

Be with your loved ones.

God of love, you were so generous, sending the presence of your Beloved to dwell among us and to tell us who you are. Encourage me during this Advent season to continue in the sharing of this loving presence through my attentiveness, given in prayer and in deeds. You who dwell within me, remind me often to let go of my busyness and my hurriedness so that I can be with others in a loving way. Convince me that "being" is as important as "doing." Thank you for your strengthening presence. Thank you for being with me. Amen.

Each of the above suggestions could be written on an index card and placed in the center of an Advent wreath. Draw one card out each day. The concluding prayer could be prayed each day after drawing the card out.

The Many Disguises of Emmanuel

Emmanuel, God-with-us,
long awaited, eagerly anticipated,
delicious dreams of royal robes,
a messiah enthroned with elegance.

False notions and easily accepted illusions.

A few open ones, full of surprise,
heard the fresh, full cry of life
echoed in the uninhabited haven,
the only place ready for a birth that was ripe.

Shepherds, sages, and scribes,
drawn by angels and stars,
discovered this divine simplicity,
then hurried from the hillside
with news that amazed them all.

But many years later the cry goes unheard,
stifled in the roar of unyielding opinions,
submerged in the noise of hasty judgments,
masked in the false folds of cultural glitter.

The Surprising One continues to come,
entering the world in endless disguise,
concealed in those we have never forgiven,
secreted in the hearts of people we despise,
found in the rejected and unacceptable,
hidden in the ones we ignore and criticize.

—Joyce Rupp

The Gift of Hope

God of all those who yearn for a glimmer of assurance on the long journey home to you, come! Come with a vast storehouse of renewed dreams, hopes, and peacefulness.

God of hope, come! Enter into my memory and remind me often of the yearning of the people of history. Stir up stories of how the ancestors hung on to your promises, how they stole hope from tiny glimmers about you, passed on from age to age. Help me to hear the loud, crying voices of the prophets who proclaimed that a new age would dawn.

God of hope, come! Enter into this heart of mine which often loses itself in self, missing the message of your encouragement because I am so entangled in the web of my own whirl of life. Enable me to not lose sight of the power of your presence or the truth of your consolation.

God of hope, come! Enter into the lives of all those I hold dear, the ones whose lives are marked with pain, struggle, and deep anxiety, those whose lives bear ongoing heartaches, those whose difficulties threaten to overwhelm them with helplessness and despair. Come and gift them with a deep belief about you and your never-ending faithfulness and companionship.

God of hope, come! Enter into every human heart that cries out for a glimpse of your love, for a sign of your welcoming presence, for a taste of your happiness. Be the one who calms the restless and gentles the ache of the human journey.

God of hope, come! Enter into this Advent season with the grace of joy and laughter. Fill faces with smiles of delight and voices with sounds of pleasure. Let this gift come from deep within. Replenish all with the joyful blessings that only your peace can bring.

God of hope, come! Be the Morning Star in our midst, the Light that can never go out, the Beacon of Hope guiding our way to you. Come into our midst and make of our lives a home, where your everlasting goodness resonates with assuring love and vigorous hope.

—Joyce Rupp

The Word Was Made Flesh

Various voices read the statements; pause for silent reflection after each statement. The Leader then offers the invitation, "Let us pray" and all give the response. In conclusion, all pray the closing prayer.

Response after each statement:

The Word was made flesh and dwelt among us (John 1:14).

Leader

—I paused on a winter cold night and felt the beauty of soft snowflakes upon my cheeks. I marveled at a presence more than mine in that moment of wonder . . .

—I visited a dying woman in the hospital. I sensed her courage and her strength in the midst of great frailty . . .

—I looked into the eyes of the clerk in the department store. They were the eyes of one who was tired and discouraged . . .

—I walked past a homeless man on the street. He held out an ungloved hand and asked me for coffee money to warm him in the cold . . .

—I opened the newspaper and saw a photo of children killed in a bombing. Parents wept over them and soldiers stood nearby with their guns . . .

—I went to a Christmas party and saw friends of long ago. We laughed and reminisced and enjoyed the moments we had known in years gone by . . .

—I spent the early morning hour in prayer, asking God to tell me the meaning of incarnation in my life . . .

—I read a letter from a single parent who still has no work. She grieves over the little she can give her children and worries about their health . . .

—I opened up the package that came in the mail. When I saw the little sprigs of fresh holly, hope sprang up in my heart . . .

—I went to church today and sang the songs of Advent yearning. I turned my heart to the God who is always in need of a better dwelling place and I begged for my transformation. . . .

All

O Word made flesh, you came to dwell among us long ago. No matter how dull and lifeless, or how happy and fulfilling our lives may be, there is always need for a deeper awareness of your hopeful presence. There are signs of your coming, signs of your continued presence, everywhere in our lives. Freshen up our vision so that we can recognize your dwelling within us and among us as we move hurriedly in this busy season of the year. May our lives be filled with love for all those who come our way. Amen.

Light Our Way

Environment: a room that can be darkened and a central, large, unlit candle. Each participant is given a small vigil light or similar candle that is fully contained so wax will not spill when the candle is carried. The ritual begins with no candles lit.

Welcome (Leader)

Welcome to this Advent ritual. In this sacred season, we remember and celebrate the gift of Divine Love who leapt from the Holy Womb into the heart of humanity. This Loving Presence became for us a source of hope, compassion, and courage. This Love Incarnate came as a light radiating compassion, a Torch bearing truth, a Beacon offering guidance.

As we welcome this Light we begin in the dark. Be attentive to darkness. Recognize that some darkness is good and nurturing. The Christ was nurtured in a womb of darkness and came forth from this blessed darkness to be a Light for us. Other darkness is destructive and bleeds love from the world. It is the darkness of war, racism, hatred, greed, and all non-loving in whatever form it takes. The Christ came to stand up to this destructive darkness and to light our path with goodness.

Let us pause now for reflection on the darkness in our world as we sit without light.

Silent Reflection in Darkness

All lighting is now extinguished, creating a room of complete darkness. The group sits in silence for 3-5 minutes.

Lighting of the Candles

After the time of silence/darkness, one central candle is lit. Then the following passage from Isaiah 9:2 is proclaimed by a reader:

> The people who walked in darkness
>   have seen a great light;
> those who lived in a land of deep darkness
> on them light has shined.

Each participant holds his/her small candle and lights it from the central candle or from light that is passed around the group. The leader then blesses the candles:

May the light of these candles we carry be a reminder of the divine radiance within us. As we hold these candles may we walk with hope and confidence in the power of our God to dispel all destructive darkness.

Sending Hope to the Four Corners of the Earth

All hold their lit candles and face east.

Leader

We face the direction of the rising sun. May each dawn offer us hope and remind us of the coming of the Christ to our world. We open our hearts to receive this Divine Light. . . . Let us now offer this Birthing Light to all in the east who need hope.

All candles are raised high, a pause of silence. Sing the chant "Light Our Way" (see Appendix):

> Light our way, Light our way,
> as we journey in the darkness.
> Light our way, Light our way,
> gift us with hope for our world.

All turn to face the south.

Leader

We face the south with its energy of growth, vitality, and abundant fruitfulness. We open our hearts to embrace the Divine Light, source of all spiritual transformation. Let us offer this Radiant Love to anyone dwelling in the south who is experiencing darkness.

All candles are raised high, a pause of silence. The chant is sung. All turn to face the west.

Leader

We face the place of the setting sun, the ending of the day. We open our hearts to receive the Divine Light that guides us in our times of

out of the ordinary

farewell. Let us offer this Divine Wisdom to all who need guidance in their darkness.

All candles are raised high, a pause of silence. Sing the chant. All turn to face the north.

Leader

We face the north with its strength and its challenge, with its natural beauty, and with its long months of wintered barrenness. We open our hearts to receive the strength of the Divine Light. Let us offer this Divine Courage of the Divine Light to all in the north who yearn for new life to sprout from their darkness.

All candles are raised high, a pause of silence. Sing the chant.

Procession and Placement of Candles

The leader then continues to move around the space with everyone following, holding their lit candles and singing the chant until arriving around the central altar or table. All place their candles on the altar or table, gathering in a circle around the candles.

Proclamations of Hope

The leader invites those present to make a one sentence statement of hope or longing such as "I hope . . ." or "I long for. . . ."

Sign of Peace

All are encouraged to share some sign of peace and hope with one another. Then the following verse from Isaiah 60:1 is proclaimed by the reader:

> Arise, shine; for your light has come,
> and the glory of [God] has risen upon you.

Close by singing the chant one more time.

Advent

29

Mary and Elizabeth

Mary and Elizabeth
two strong women
whose wombs
carried two strong men

Mary and Elizabeth
two hospitable women
with wombs wide, full
of grace and conversion

Mary and Elizabeth,
two generous women,
nurturing nests,
embracing seedling life
in their bodies' secret homes

Mary and Elizabeth,
two loving women,
blessing one another
with the grace of affection,
strength of communion

Mary and Elizabeth,
did they know the dance
within their wombs
might change a hurting heart,
transform a languished life

Mary and Elizabeth,
two holy women
wombs gestating goodness,
sources of nurturing grace
yeast for every inner birthing

—Joyce Rupp

All Saints' Day/
All Souls' Day

Who Are the Saints?

> The saints are those who, in some partial way,
> embody—literally incarnate—the challenge of faith
> in their time and place. In doing so, they open a
> path that others might follow.
>
> —Robert Ellsberg

I have always been drawn to the Feast of All Saints. It is a time to remember with gratitude all those persons whose goodness has inspired me in my beliefs and given me courage to act on what I believe. It is a day to acknowledge that these holy men and women have helped me find my own potential for goodness.

I think of "saints" as not only those women and men who have been canonized by the church, but all people whose lives reflect the goodness of God. Saints are not perfect people. They have their faults, idiosyncrasies, and weaknesses. They have their own struggles and difficulties. Even the canonized ones are noted to have been difficult to live with because of some of their unique mannerisms. Yet, the saints are people of integrity. They have a central focus at the core of their lives: the love of God. They consistently choose to act out of that central reality, no matter how ordinary or extraordinary their lives may be.

One of the finest books I have used for daily inspiration is Robert Ellsberg's *All Saints.* * In this book of 365 daily reflections on saints, Ellsberg notes that the "communion of saints" was a vivid reality for the early Christians. They would gather at the gravesites of martyrs to remember the martyrs' witness to the gospel and commemorate the anniversary of their deaths. This ritual was the seed for the future feast of All Saints' Day. As we celebrate this feast on November 1, we gather to commemorate not just martyrs or people we might tend to put on spiritual pedestals, but all those people who have drawn us to God because of who they were and how they lived. All Saints' Day is an excellent opportunity for us to be re-inspired by their virtuous lives and to cherish the union we have with them.

* *All Saints, Daily Reflections on Saints, Prophets, and Witnesses for Our Time.* Robert Ellsberg. Crossroad Publ. Co., 1997.

out of the ordinary

Whether we know it or not, we transmit the presence
of everyone we have ever known, as though by being
in each other's presence we exchange our cells, pass
on some of our life force, and then we go on carrying
that other person in our body, not unlike springtime
when certain plants in fields we walk through attach
their seeds in the form of small burrs to our socks,
our pants, our caps, as if to say "Go on, take us with
you, carry us to root in another place." This is how
we survive long after we are dead. This is why it is
important who we become, because we pass it on.

—Natalie Goldberg

Leader

God of our ancestors, today we gather to our hearts all those who
have influenced our lives with their love and goodness. Although
they have passed on to the other side of this life, their lives continue
to affect who we are and what we do. Like the sound of a bell
resounding in the welcoming air, so has the goodness of these holy
ones resonated in our lives. Thank you for these ancestors and the
bond we have with them.

Reader 1

Read Revelation 7:9-14 (the great multitude robed in white).

Response

A song of the beatitudes, or God's faithfulness, or similar theme is sung.

Leader

Let us listen now as we are invited to remember various groups of
our spiritual ancestors. After each group is mentioned, we will have a
quiet time so you can name aloud or silently anyone you want to
mention from that particular group. A bell will be rung after the
names have been given for each group to remind us of how their
goodness has resonated in our lives.

All Saints' Day/All Souls' Day

Reader 2

We now call to mind our spiritual ancestors:

1. Let us remember the ones who lived and loved deeply, who found the source of their inner strength from you, the Divine Beloved. . . . (Pause for individual names to be spoken; after the names are spoken, a chiming bell is then rung; all listen to its resonance. This process is used after each of the following groups of ancestors is named.)

2. Let us remember **the light-filled ones**, who enkindled our spirits with their teachings and the spark of their beliefs. . . .

3. Let us remember **the risk-takers**, who faced their fears and took action, who sought justice even though they had to pay a price for it. . . .

4. Let us remember **the vulnerable ones** who allowed us to care for them, to be with them in their time of need. . . .

5. Let us remember **the faith-filled ones** who brought us to the Holy One, who led us, by their words and example, into deeper relationship with God. . . .

6. Let us remember **the brave ones** who walked through their struggles with hope, who taught us how to trust and have confidence during our times of sorrow and difficulty. . . .

7. Let us remember **the great lovers of life**, whose humor and enthusiasm lifted our spirits and brought us joy. . . .

8. Let us remember **the nurturers**, who birthed us physically or spiritually, who gave us sustenance by their caring presence. . . .

    Are there other groups or individuals we wish to remember?
    (Pause for the naming of these spiritual ancestors.)

All (or Leader)

Sacred One, Giver and Sustainer of life,
thank you for the holy ones whom we have known.
As they embrace you in the white-robed home of eternity,
we give you thanks for them.
May our lives model their virtues.
May our hearts resonate with their goodness. Amen.

The prayer service concludes with ringing of bells. These bells can be the church bells and/or bells that participants have brought with them.

out of the ordinary

Celebrating the Radiant Light of the Holy Ones

A vigil light or a candle of similar nature is needed for each person who is present. An explanation about "saints" (canonized and uncanonized) being good people should be given (see "Who Are the Saints?"). The ritual begins with all of the candles, unlit, placed in a circle on an altar or table. Set one central candle in the middle of these candles. If possible, all present are seated in a circle around the altar or table. Begin in as much darkness as possible. After a short period of silence, the chant is sung for three or four minutes.

Chant: Holy One*

The central candle is now lit.

Prayer

Divine Light, Radiant Holy One, Light of all Lights,
we call upon all the saints to be with us.
We remember how each one brought a touch of your light
   into our world.
We recall how each one reflected the radiance of your goodness.
We recount their loving deeds and rejoice in their faithfulness.

Reading: Matthew 5:14-16

"You are the light of the world. A city built on a hill cannot be hid. No one after lighting a lamp puts it under the bushel basket, but on the lampstand, and it gives light to all in the house. In the same way, let your light shine before others, so that they may see your good works and give glory to [God]. . . ."

Lighting of Candles

Everyone present is invited to light a candle for a saint who inspired them and to briefly tell what quality they most appreciated about this person's life. As the candle is lit, the person speaks: "I light this candle for _____. I am grateful for how he (she) reflected the Divine Light by _____." Some may prefer to simply light the candle in silence and stand for a moment, honoring the memory of their particular saint.

All Saints' Day/All Souls' Day

Silent Gratitude

After the lighting of each individual candle, all stand and join hands in silent thanksgiving. The leader invites the group to this silence with the following prayer.

Leader

As we stand around these candles with joined hands, we remember the powerful communion we have with the saints, both canonized and uncanonized. Let us pause in silence to be grateful for all we have learned from them and for the ways in which they have helped us reflect the goodness of God.

Invitation to Let Our Light Shine *(Be seated.)*

The leader then invites the participants to think about what quality of goodness they most want to reflect in their lives.

And so, my friends, let us renew our intention to let our light shine, to follow in the footsteps of the saints. I invite you now to name how you hope to have the goodness of God reflected in your life in the coming year.

Each one now proclaims his/her intention: "I will let the light of my . . . (honesty, justice, kindness, generosity, patience, etc.) shine brightly."

Joyful Conclusion

Chant "Those Who Brought Light,"* or a jubilant song such as "I Danced in the Morning," or "Blest Are They," or "When The Saints Come Marching In."

*See Appendix—Chants

out of the ordinary

A Personal Ritual for All Saints' Day

Besides the communal prayer suggested in this section, here is one that you can pray individually.* On or before November 1, take time for the following prayer experience. Have near you a small container, such as a cup, bowl, basket, or small box, and at least thirty small pieces of paper. An index card cut into fours is a good size.

1. Begin by reflecting on one of these scripture passages: Revelation 7:9-14, Matthew 5:1-15, or another passage that speaks to you about being a follower of Jesus, filled with his qualities and goodness.

2. Sit quietly. Ask for divine guidance as you ponder saints who have drawn you to deeper faith, to a closer union with God. These might be people you have known personally, through scripture or history; they may be spiritual and theological authors, poets or singers—anyone who has inspired you and stirred your desire to be faithful to the Christ-like goodness within you.

3. As persons and names come to your mind, take the small pieces of paper and write a name on each one. As you do so, place these names in the container. As each one goes in, whisper "thank you" for the gift of that person's goodness. (More people may come to your mind later on; if so, continue to add these names to the container.)

4. After the names are in the container, pray this prayer or one of your own:

Thank you, Heart of all Goodness, for each of these saints who have been a part of my life in some way. Thank you for their witness and inspiration. Thank you for how their life encourages me to live my own in a better way. I renew my dedication to you and pray that their qualities of goodness will continue to grow and mature in me. May your love shine through me so that one day I, too, may be counted among the white-robed ones who stand before your throne.

5. Keep the container of names on a prayer altar, a desk, table, or any place where you will see them. Each day of November draw

out one name. Look lovingly at the name. Remember the person whom that name signifies. Ask yourself: What does this person's life teach me about the goodness of God and about how to live my life well? (You may want to write this quality on the back of the paper with the name on it.) After you have recognized this quality, place the name alongside the container. Conclude each day with the prayer above or one of your own.

6. Each day, try to live the quality of the saint whose name and life you pondered. (You might want to carry the name with you for the day as a reminder of this and place it alongside the container of names at the day's end.)

7. At the close of the month, gather all the names strewn around the container and hold them to your heart. Pray that your life will continue to contain the virtues of these saints. You may want to write these names in your journal or place the list in a picture frame where they will remind you of their qualities of goodness.

* This could be done as a family with each member writing names and placing them in a container that sits on the family table. Draw one name out at meal time. The family member who wrote the name describes the quality of goodness. If other family members know the saint, they add other qualities of goodness that they find in the saint. The names are placed on a small plate next to the container and remain there for the month of November. If family members find it difficult to all be at meals at the same time, each one can draw a name during the day and follow with steps 5 and 6.

out of the ordinary

The Blessing of the Saints

(A Guided Visualization)

This reflection is best used when one person slowly reads and leads another person or a group through the visualization. Begin by finding a comfortable place and peaceful bodily position for the visualization.

Begin by relaxing and quieting your mind and body.

Pay attention to your breath; notice how the breath comes in and goes out. . . .

Let yourself feel contentment, joy, peace. Allow a sense of deep trust to fill you. . . .

Go within to a deeper part of yourself.

Picture yourself in a place that seems like a blessing place to you. . . .

Make yourself comfortable in this place. . . .

See the outlines of white-robed figures in the distance. . . .

They are moving toward you with an easy flow of goodness and grace.

You can feel the power of their love and their belief in you. . . .

Each of those coming to you has been a great blessing for you.

The white-robed figures are coming to you, one by one. . . .

As they come to you, notice how they look at you with love, satisfaction, belief, trust, hope. . . .

One of your life-givers comes—someone who nurtured your body or your spirit.

This life-giver comes to you and blesses you. . . .

Next, one of your mentors or teachers who has given you wisdom comes.

This wise one also blesses you. . . .

Now one of your challengers comes, someone who urged you to take risks and to stretch beyond your secure place. Let this challenging one bless you. . . .

Then all those who especially helped you to become the person you are today come to you. These beloved ones bless you. . . .

Look at all of these white-robed ones gathered around you, extending love to you. . . .

Thank them for all they have done for you. . . . Now bid these special ones farewell.

With all the blessings in your heart, now visualize yourself standing up with your arms outstretched toward the universe. See yourself moving slowly in a circle, facing all four directions as you turn. Your love goes forth from you to all of creation. Let yourself be a blessing for the world.

Now, slowly come back to this time and place.

After the visualization, take some time for responses to the meditation. These could be through dialogue, painting, journaling, etc.

A Personal Prayer for All Souls' Day

> Do not withhold kindness
> even from the dead.

> —Sirach 7:33

The following could be prayed by anyone who feels alienated or not at peace with someone who has died.

1. Have before you a photo of the person who has died.

2. Recall your differences, the situations and events that sparked the alienation.

3. Write about some of these difficult memories. You may even want to write a dialogue with the person who has died.

4. Hold these memories out to Jesus, the healer. Allow him to take these memories and hurts from you.

5. Visualize Jesus welcoming you and healing you from these memories and hurts.

6. Pray for peace for the one who has died. Envision this person being at rest, at home in the arms of God. (Or visualize Jesus taking this person by the hand and welcoming him or her home.)

7. Allow peace to permeate your mind and heart. Rest in the comfort of God's love.

A Communal Prayer for All Souls' Day

Leader

We unite in compassion with all souls who have died and who may not yet be at peace. Let us pray for (*pause after each naming for silent prayer*):

. . . those who have taken their own lives or caused their own deaths,

. . . those who died due to their violence or brutal aggression,

. . . those who failed to reconcile their anger and remained alienated,

. . . those who have been executed for heinous crimes they committed,

. . . those who fought death and refused to be comforted,

. . . those whose ego-focused decisions led to the deaths of others,

. . . those killed in car accidents caused by their own substance abuse or recklessness,

. . . those who raged against others and died with hate in their hearts,

. . . Are there other souls who died in distress for whom we wish to pray? (*Pause as these persons are named, silently or aloud.*)

Let us pray:

Merciful One, it is not for us to judge those who have died. Rather, we come to you with the assurance of your great compassion. We unite with these wounded brothers and sisters of ours and believe that you draw all to your forgiving heart. May the love we bear be encouragement for all souls winging their way home to you. Thank you for your unconditional love for all you have created. Amen.

Birthdays

Birthdays

Each birthday I am drawn to reflect on the amazing treasure of being alive. I am astounded by the aspect of existence, I marvel that I am fortunate enough to get to dance through a little segment of the universe's history. I pause to re-enter wonder, to be amazed again at how my life took form from the union of my mother's egg and my father's sperm. My birthday is a good opportunity to remember not to take this gift of life for granted (which I can easily do on my busy days).

I also like to re-examine my life on my birthday. I wander through the many experiences of my past year and I ask myself: Who was I a year ago? Am I different today? How have I grown? Who and what has shaped my consciousness? Am I a more loving, kinder, more gracious human being now? What do I long for and what seems yet unfinished? Who are the significant people in my life and how has our journey together been? All these questions and many more circle around me on my birthday. It is usually an energizing, enjoyable, and sometimes challenging reflection.

Then I look at my place in the universe. I see how small I am and how vast the cosmos is. This increases my sense of absolute wonderment, to think that I even exist at all. It also calls me to look closely to see if I am an active ingredient in the positive transformation of the Earth, to see if I am caring for and aware of the needs of the planet and the creatures that dwell on it and in it.

Gratitude normally takes up a large segment of this time of pondering. I see for whom and what I have to give thanks. I savor all that I can because I know that the life I've been given the past year is provision for the next one. Even during the difficult and pain-filled years, I have found much for which to be grateful. It's really just a matter of looking very closely.

Finally, I conclude my birthday reflection by writing a simple statement of hope for my coming year. I end with a prayer of gratitude and trust in the Holy One's mercy and kindness.

A Birthday Reflection

I look back upon the past year, through the many ups and downs, and I gather my significant memories—people, events, inner stirrings, dreams, jolts, joys, heartaches, etc.—all that touched my life in any sort of special way.

As I look over my year:

I am especially grateful for . . .

I am amazed at . . .

I am puzzled by . . .

I wish that . . .

As I look toward the coming year:

I long for . . .

I hope that . . .

I trust . . .

I promise . . .

I ask . . .

Now pause and visualize a messenger of God drawing near to you. This messenger bears a blessing of God for your coming year. Receive the blessing from the messenger. Spend some time in quiet, allowing the blessing to permeate your entire being.

To conclude this reflection, write a short prayer in your journal or on a paper that you will keep and refer to each month on the date of your birthday (e.g., if your birthday is the tenth of May, on the tenth of each month you would read your birthday prayer and remember the blessing that was given to you). Now go and celebrate!

Birthday Blessing

May you sip contentedly
from the fragrant wine of your life.

May you stretch eagerly
into the opening light of each new day.

May you discover kernels of wisdom
hidden in unwanted experiences.

May you find comfort and consolation
when you are hurting.

May you know the protection
and guidance of your angels.

May you hear the tender voice
of the Beloved calling to you
in the deepest part of your being.

May you have a soul friend
whose unconditional love
gives you courage to keep growing.

May you be a bearer of loving kindness
when you meet those who suffer.

May you gather your daily blessings
to your heart and relish their presence.

May you never give up seeking greater peace
for yourself and for your world.

May you go to sleep each evening
aware of being held in the embrace
of a merciful and welcoming God.

May you hear the marvelous music
singing in your soul every moment,
lauding the exquisite gift of being alive.

—Joyce Rupp

out of the ordinary

A Ritual for Aging

For those age 60 and older

> O God, from my youth you have taught me,
> and I still proclaim your wondrous deeds.
> So even to old age and gray hairs,
> O God, do not forsake me,
> until I proclaim your might
> to all the generations to come.

> —Psalm 71:17-18

1. Look at photos of yourself from infancy to the present time.

2. Ponder a photo of yourself as an infant or very young child. Rejoice in the gift of your life. Be amazed at the fact you were born.

3. Ponder a photo of yourself as a youth. Be grateful for all the energy you had.

4. Ponder a photo of yourself in your 20s or 30s. Be grateful for your ability to work, to be active.

5. Ponder a photo of yourself in your 40s or 50s. Be grateful for the questions and inner changes that occurred for you during those years.

6. Ponder a more recent photo of yourself. Think about who and what you now most cherish in your life. Be grateful for who you have become.

7. Line up the photos by age, look at the change in yourself. Think of how "life" has changed you. List your greatest joys, successes, blessings. List your greatest struggles, disappointments, hurts.

8. Write a summary paragraph describing the person you are now.

9. Close by creating a psalm based on your life experience of aging.

Birthdays

Christmas

Dancing God

Dancing God
passionate leap
of creative energy
skipping among the stars
waltzing on rivers
birthing a universe

Dancing God
tumbling from somewhere
into Jewish territory
whirling Spirit
seeding Mary's womb
with alluring divinity

Dancing God
uncontainable grandeur
kicking and rolling
in Mary's flesh
while untamed cousin
echoes the dance
in aunt Elizabeth

Dancing God
spark of angel's song
shepherds hurrying
like whirling dervishes
gasping in awe
at a surprising child

Dancing God
still passionate today
dynamic movement of love
wooing our hearts
toward oneness and peace
in a tear-stained world

Dance on, Passionate God,
we are your dance now
teach us the tune
show us the steps
it is Christmas
it is time to dance

—Joyce Rupp

A Christmas Blessing

—May there be harmony in all your relationships. May sharp words, envious thoughts, and hostile feelings be dissolved.

—May you give and receive love generously. May this love echo in your heart like the joy of church bells on a clear December day.

—May each person who comes into your life be greeted as another Christ. May the honor given the Babe of Bethlehem be that which you extend to every guest who enters your presence.

—May the hope of this sacred season settle in your soul. May it be a foundation of courage for you when times of distress occupy your inner land.

—May the wonder and awe that fills the eyes of children be awakened within you. May it lead you to renewed awareness and appreciation of whatever you too easily take for granted.

—May the bonds of love for one another be strengthened as you gather with your family and friends around the table of festivity and nourishment.

—May you daily open the gift of your life and be grateful for the hidden treasures it contains.

—May the coming year be one of good health for you. May you have energy and vitality. May you care well for your body, mind, and spirit.

—May you keep your eye on the Star within you and trust this Luminescent Presence to guide and direct you each day.

—May you go often to the Bethlehem of your heart and visit the One who offers you peace. May you bring this peace into our world.

—Joyce Rupp

Keeping Watch in the Night

shepherds
keeping watch in the night,
close to the grassy slopes,
at home in the darkness,
a listening presence
in the midnight emptiness

shepherds
keeping watch in the night,
terrified by a voice
not heard before,
not supposed to be there

shepherds
keeping watch in the night,
alarmed by powerful light,
up-ending their security

but they did not run away

they stayed in the dark
and listened,
stretched their ears
to the unknown voice

and the voice said:
"do not be afraid.
stay in this dark place
and listen.
I have wonderful news:
the Hoped-for-One,
the Birthing you've longed for
in the depths of your soul,
has come, oh yes, has come!"

The watchers of the night,
the keepers of the Inner Longing,
enchanted by music of the skies,
hurried on midnight feet
and found the One who waited

unlike what they'd expected
and surprisingly beautiful,
all those night watches,
and the deep Inner Longing,
now they knew
now they knew

—Joyce Rupp

The Singing Tree

It may be that some little root
of the sacred tree still lives.
Nourish it then,
that it may leaf and bloom
and fill with singing birds.

—Black Elk

I cannot recall exactly when I first heard the singing tree. I do know it was in the heart of winter time. It was one of those tired, frozen days when any sound of life is a welcome respite from the grayness. I was bundled up in layers of clothes, beginning my regular walk in early dawn. I was a little later than usual on that particular morning as I opened the door and walked down the driveway to the sidewalk. The wintry morning was quiet except for my boots crunching loudly on the endless snow as I walked past the tall spruce tree.

As I passed the tree it suddenly came alive with song. Startled, I stopped to listen. Deep inside the thickly branched tree the sparrows had been awakened by some inner alarm clock. These little feathered creatures that I could not see began heralding the dawn with their symphony of cheeps, quickly filling the gray day with the sparkle of their voices. I stood there amazed, my heart transformed. A smile came as I pondered that usually silent tree now full of hidden music. The cares and worries of the winter day immediately lost their layers of burden and urgency as I set out on my walk with a lighter heart and a renewed sense of purpose and vitality.

As I walked along that morning I thought of how everyone needs a singing tree in their life for those gray-burdened days, for those just-put-one-step-in-front-of-the-other days, for those let's-just-get-this-over-with days, for those I-can't-take-much-more-of-this days. We all need a tree full of sparrow cheeps to lift our hearts into hope and to remind us of the surprising beauty of life.

To all I say this Christmas: look for the singing tree in your life. It may be the squeals and laughter of children or the guffaws of friends enjoying a good story. It may be the quiet wind in the willows or the voice of a loved one calling to say hello. It may be the chorus of glorias heard at a church service or the tinkle of chimes on the back porch. It may be the voice of God in your heart telling you of your own goodness by a well satisfied feeling, or it may be a zillion little sparrows hidden in a wintered spruce tree chirping their first song of the dawn. This Christmas, listen closely. You may hear a singing tree and your heart be filled with joy.

The Christ Is Born Again

For years I was held in a tiny cell. My only human contact was with my torturers. For two and a half of those years I did not experience the glance of a human face, see a green leaf. My only company was the cockroaches and mice. The only daylight that entered my cell was through a small opening at the top of one wall. For eight months I had my hands and feet tied. On Christmas Eve, the door to my cell opened, and the guard tossed in a crumpled piece of paper. I moved as best I could to pick up the paper. It said simply, "Constantina, do not be discouraged, we know you are alive." It was signed "Monica" and had the Amnesty International candle on it. These words saved my life and my sanity. Eight months later I was set free.

—Constantina Coronel,
released prisoner from Uruguay,
Amnesty International Newsletter, 1996

two thousand years ago
a Child cries in the night
songs of silver-throated angels
beckon wild-eyed shepherds
running on trembling feet
beneath the dancing Star of joy

two thousand years later
another cry in the night
a woman named Constantina
rots in tortured prison cell
only a sliver of sun
and never a glimpse of green

a message comes
on Christmas eve
not with silver throats

or gleaming Star
but on crumpled note
amid cockroaches and rodents

words of assurance
balm for a despairing heart
and the Christ
is born again
in the power of hope
and the candle of compassion

—Joyce Rupp

A Christmas of Contrasts

I receive cards and letters from dear ones.

> . . . There are many who have no one to love them.

I sit down to a Christmas dinner, a table of abundance.

> . . . There are those who long for just a small portion of food and find none.

I feel love and goodness from those around me.

> . . . There are people terrorized by death squads and tortured in prisons.

I open my many gifts, most of which are not needed.

> . . . There are those who have no gifts to give or receive.

I move freely from home to home choosing whom I see and visit.

> . . . There are visually impaired, physically challenged, chronically ill persons who cannot move easily.

I am welcomed by friends, family, and acquaintances.

> . . . There are persons who are mocked, ridiculed, disdained, or ignored because of their race and religion.

I return to the security of my home.

> . . . There are countless homeless who have no dwelling place to which they can return.

This Christmas, will I recognize God's presence in my world? Will I look beyond my own comfortable, cozy space and find God dwelling among the many who are lost, lonely, ill, neglected, forgotten? Will their presence in the world make any difference in how I celebrate the Holy One's coming to dwell in my midst? Will I see the love of God shining through the windowed hearts of Earth's people? Will I hear the truth told long ago of this Beloved's kindness toward all? Will I hold these people in my heart this Christmas? Will I let them touch my prayer and my celebration?

Christmas

A Blessing of Angels

If you look into the scriptures you will find that angels encircled the entire life of Jesus, from the angel's invitation asking Mary to welcome Jesus in her womb to the blessed moment of an angel announcing his being raised from the dead.

May the angel of the annunciation bless you, inviting you daily to awaken to the God-life within you.

May the angel of Joseph's dreams bless you, stirring your spirit to trust the many ways that Mystery whispers to you.

May the angel of birthing bless you, calling forth wonder, awe, and gratitude for all that has helped you to become your true self.

May the angel of Bethlehem-songs bless you, tickling your soul with laughter and joy, heralding hope and good tidings to you.

May the angel of the journey to Egypt bless you, guiding and protecting you as you travel the inner and outer roads of your life.

May the angel of desert wilderness bless you, bringing courage when you experience bleak, intense searching and struggle.

May the angel of prayer bless you, gathering you closely to the divine Beloved who longs for your embrace.

May the angel of children on the lap of Jesus bless you, helping you to see the beauty and freedom of your inner child.

May the angel of the agony in the garden bless you, offering you solace in your times of tribulation.

May the angel at the tomb of resurrection bless you with faith, assuring your faith and trust that all shall be well.*

—Joyce Rupp

*The chant "Angels Before Me" could be sung as a closing to this prayer.

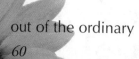

out of the ordinary

Difficult Times

In Difficult Times

Consoling God,
be a source of serenity for me
when struggles and difficulties
threaten to overwhelm me.

God of hope,
assure me of your unconditional love
when I doubt myself
or question the worth of my life.

Truth-bringing God,
encourage me to embrace you
during those times when I get lost
in the lies of my weakness.

Compassionate God,
hold me to your heart
when I feel helpless
in the face of the world's pain.

Light-filled God,
keep me ever close to you
during those moments
when bleakness surrounds my life.

Comforting God,
shelter me under your wings
when I am engulfed in sadness
and overcome with distress.

God of peace,
you are the center of my life,
a strong refuge of peace
in the whirlwind of my pain.
I look to you for strength
and a constant assurance of hope.

—Joyce Rupp

A Haunting Question

"Are you the one who is to come,
or are we to wait for another?"

—Matthew 11:3

This poignant question from the heart of John the Baptist in prison was carried by his disciples to Jesus. John had looked into the eyes of Jesus, had touched him, baptized him, known him to be filled with goodness. Yet, in a moment of crisis, in a time of dread, during long weeks of isolation and pain, that huge crying-out question leapt up in John. It seared his throat and gasped for an answer. Strong words pressed against his faltering faith: "Tell me that you are the one. Tell me that you are."

We also have our John the Baptist moments. They come when we are in the prison of our own life struggles of despair, discouragement, and desolation. Like John, we can trust and love, believe and hope, and know that God is real and near. But when those terrifying times of emptiness and pain come, no matter how strong the love we have known, we can also cry out, hesitate to hope, and question what we have believed: "What is this all about? Where are you, God, when I need you most?" Like John the Baptist, we send the plea: "Tell me that you are the one. Send assurance that my hope in you is valid."

The response that Jesus sent back to John in prison is also the one that is given to us in our difficult times: "Go and tell John what you hear and see: the blind receive their sight, the lame walk, the lepers are cleansed, the deaf hear, the dead are raised, and the poor have good news brought to them. And blessed is anyone who takes no offense at me" (Mt 11:4-6). In other words, Jesus was reminding John to recall what he had seen in the past and not to doubt it. Jesus was saying, "Don't let your emotions overpower you. Recall the goodness you have experienced in our relationship in the past. Trust my love for you even if I am not rescuing you from your prison of troubles."

Jesus says much the same to us: "Remember that I have been with you as the source of life and love. Look at those who stand by you. My

Spirit is alive in them. I love you through their kindness and care. Notice the little, overlooked gifts of life that are in each day. I can assure you that I care for you by the love that comes to you through even the tiniest thing that brings you comfort and relief."

God is with us. We need to keep on discovering how this loving presence is a part of our lives. When we doubt this presence, we can send our messengers of prayer and a listening heart to God and wait for the reply. It will probably come in an unanticipated insight or through an unexpected person. Like John the Baptist in prison, we voice our question. We send our messengers. And then, we wait, trusting that there will be a response.

A Prayer to Be Freed From Tizzies*

Dear God,
you who did not invent tizzies,
be with me when I get caught
in the wild worrying of my mind,
and the needless scurrying around
in my fearful heart.

Trip me up when I fret and stew
so I can see the trap of tizzies,
with their schemes to keep me
bunched up in stress and strain.

Let me fall headfirst into the truth
of your never-ending presence,
wrap your kind arms around me
and calm my doubts and fears.

Shout loudly in my spiritual ear
when my nerves get knotted,
my mind feels cramped,
and my stomach screams.

It may be difficult,
but do try to get my full attention,
because tizzies are not healthy,
and they definitely chase peace
out the front door of my heart.

Dear God, you did not invent tizzies,
I did,
and only I can send them on their way,
and I will,
if you strengthen me
to let go of my anxious hold
on what is nonessential.

—Joyce Rupp

* A tizzy is "a state of frenzied excitement or distraction, especially over some trivial matter" (Webster's New Unabridged Dictionary).

Searching for Oneself

Good Shepherd, who finds the lost one,
the "me" I have known has disappeared.

Will I ever recover the person I have been?
Will I ever find and feel good about myself again?
Will I discover who I am and who I am becoming?

Protect me in this great vulnerability.
Assure me that I will come home to myself,
even though "my self" may be different.

Silence my impatience.
Calm my worry.
Restore my joy.
Solace my distress.
Help me to befriend my new self
with tender hope and welcoming love.

—Joyce Rupp

Hope Continues to Bloom

yesterday I went to view the dead,
instead I found the living.
my inner fibers stirred wonderingly
as I discovered green beans in abundance.

all those long, heat-filled days,
over a month without moisture,
and there those green beans were,
blooming and bearing bountifully.

I stood and gazed at their resilience,
remembering my own dry days inside
when it seemed not a green bean was left
on the withered vine of my scorched life.

I pondered my own long stretch of drought
without a soothing drop of consoling life.
I saw that my roots, too, had gone down deep,
seeking the secret soil of endurance.

I know now that hope continues to bloom
in the valley of desolation and dryness,
that within my arid, breathless space,
greening life has power over death.

standing before my inner garden
I see how faithfully the unfelt Source
took care of me, feeding my roots
as I sipped unknowingly.

—Joyce Rupp

Blessing Before Surgery

In her book Kitchen Table Wisdom, *Dr. Rachel Naomi Remen describes how she asks her patients to bring a stone (small enough to fit in the palm of one's hand) to the hospital when they come in for surgery. She asks the patient to invite a small group of family members and/or friends who have a "heart bond" with him or her to come the night before surgery. That evening they gather around the bedside and each tells a story of a significant time when he or she needed strength and found it. As each one concludes her or his story, she or he names a quality from that life event and says something like, "I put encouragement into this stone," or "I put hope into this stone." The stone is then passed on to the next person who continues the process. The stone then becomes the patient's "courage stone." This ritual incorporates the "courage stone" into a blessing.*

Leader

1. As the patient holds the stone, the leader begins by asking those gathered to repeat the words of Psalm 18:2:

> [God] is my rock, my fortress, and my deliverer,
> my God, my rock in whom I take refuge.

Leader *(the patient continues to hold the stone)*

This stone has been a part of the universe for untold years. It is a symbol of strength and endurance. As each of us here holds this stone, we will bless it as a courage stone for you while we tell you stories of strength from our lives. Let us each pause to think about a time in our life when we longed for strength and found it in our time of need.

2. The leader then holds the stone and tells his or her story of strength, ending with a statement such as, "And so, _____(name of patient), I bless this stone with the gift of courage (or another quality, such as hope, humor, faith, peace)." Then the leader hands the stone to the next person with the invitation to continue the storytelling and the blessing.

out of the ordinary

3. After each one around the bedside has held the stone, told their story, and blessed the stone, it is then placed in the patient's hand. All those around the bedside now place their hands on some part of the patient while the leader prays the following blessing:

> May the divine Spirit give attentiveness and guidance to the surgical staff.
>
> May you trust in your body's ability to heal.
>
> May you have compassion for any part of your body that experiences pain or discomfort.
>
> May you befriend your fears and be freed from all anxiety.
>
> May you be at peace.
>
> We send our love and our vitality to you. Receive this loving energy from our hearts to yours and be strengthened for your journey toward healing.

4. Conclude by each one present extending some gesture of love to the patient (a hug, kiss, gentle bow, sign of cross on forehead, a gentle touch of the hand on the very frail, etc.).

For a Loved One Who Is Dying

Compassionate God,
as heart-aching as it is to let go of my loved one,
it is unfair to hold ____* back.
_____ is nearing the opening gate
to the other side of this life
where you will welcome him (her) home.

My dear one's soul is ripening
for the journey to you, great Mystery.
_____'s body grows weaker and more frail.
Soon the soul will be free to go.

Thank you for all that my loved one
has meant to me and to others.
Thank you for the loving memories
I will have long after _____ is gone.

Help me to trust
that you will support and care for me
when I no longer have the gift
of my loved one's presence.

May this dear person be confident
of your enduring love for him (her).
May the peace, that only you can give,
fill his (her) spirit and ease all concern.

May my loved one be given inner strength
to peacefully enter the realm of new life.
May I be generous in my final farewell
and give my loved one the blessing of goodbye.

Ancient One, receive this dear one
whom you loaned to me for a time.
Thank you for the blessedness of _____,
whom I now return to you with gratitude.

* name of loved one

out of the ordinary

Blessing of One Who Draws Near to Death

Those who have loved and cherished the dying person gather around the bedside. Throughout the blessing, those gathered gently touch the patient. As each part of the body is blessed, the hand of one of those present is placed on that particular part of the patient's body and remains there as the blessing and remembrances are shared.

Gathering Prayer

Leader

_____ (name of dying person), our beloved one, we gather to send you forth on the wings of love. We join with you and give you our love as you face the great mystery of life and death. We free you to take leave of us as your time nears. We cradle your love in our hearts and in our memories. You will remain a part of us always. We gather here to bless you for your journey home and to express our gratitude for what you have given to us by your presence in our lives.

Each of the following blessings is prayed by the leader who then invites those present to tell how this part of the body was a gift for the dying person and for those who were a part of his or her life. After each blessing all are invited to speak the response.

Leader

_____, we are going to bless your body. It has housed a wonderful spirit for many years and been a gift both to you and to us. Thank you for this privilege of blessing you.

Blessing of the Head

We bless your head, _____. Thank you for the ways that you have influenced our lives by your beliefs, attitudes, and values. Thank you for sharing your hopes and dreams. We especially thank your head and you for . . . (*those gathered now share specific things*).

Response: "You will always be a part of our hearts. Go in peace."

Blessing of the Eyes

We bless your eyes, _____. We are grateful for what these eyes have seen in bringing you joy and happiness. We are thankful for the times when these eyes have looked upon us with love. We especially thank your eyes and you for . . . (*those gathered now share specific things*).

Response: "You will always be a part of our hearts. Go in peace."

Blessing of the Ears

We bless your ears, _____. Thank you for the ways that they have been attuned to both the outer and the inner world. Thank you for the times you have listened to us. We especially thank your ears and you for . . . (*those gathered now share specific things*).

Response: "You will always be a part of our hearts. Go in peace."

Blessing of the Mouth

We bless your mouth, _____. This mouth has been the carrier of your wisdom. Thank you for words of courage and kindness that you have spoken to us. Thank you for the truths you gave to us. We especially thank your mouth and you for . . . (*those gathered now share specific things*).

Response: "You will always be a part of our hearts. Go in peace."

Blessing of the Hands

We bless your hands. Your hands have been a source of welcome and of help in countless ways. We offer our gratitude for all that these hands have done. We especially thank your hands and you for . . . (*those gathered now share specific things*).

Response: "You will always be a part of our hearts. Go in peace."

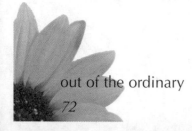

out of the ordinary

Blessing of the Sexual Organs

If the dying person is a woman who has birthed children, someone's hand is placed over her stomach area.

We bless your womb, recalling how wondrously it was filled with life. We thank your womb for the child(ren) it carried, nurtured, and brought forth. We especially thank your womb and you for . . . (*those gathered now share specific things*).

If the dying person is a man who is a father, someone's hand could be placed above the groin area.

We bless your genitalia and give thanks for the seed of life which you gave to your child(ren). We especially thank your genitalia and you for . . . (*those gathered now share specific things*).

If the dying person has not borne children, hands are placed above the breasts or groin area.

We bless your sexuality. Your femininity (or masculinity) gave passion and color to your life. Thank you for your sexuality which enhanced your life and brought enjoyment to you. We thank you and your sexuality for . . . (*those gathered now share specific things*).

Response: "You will always be a part of our hearts. Go in peace."

Blessing of the Feet

We bless your feet. You have stood and walked on these feet since your youth. These feet have journeyed through many of life's ups and downs. We thank you and your feet for . . . (*those gathered now share specific things*).

Response: "You will always be a part of our hearts. Go in peace."

Blessing of the Heart

We bless your heart. This heart has pulsed with life. It has given and received love. This heart has contained many emotional bonds with those gathered here. It has given you energy to live. We thank your heart and you for . . . (*those gathered now share specific things*).

Response: "You will always be a part of our hearts. Go in peace."

Other parts of the body could also be blessed, e.g., someone for whom life has been particularly difficult, the shoulders could be blessed and thanked for the heavy loads of life they've sustained.

Leader

We now extend our hands over you, gathering the love in our hearts and extending it to you as fully as possible. May our love surround you and fill you with strength and courage.

All extend their hands over the dying person. Then the following prayer is prayed by the leader:

> May the angels of eternal life draw you into the embrace of the divine Presence.
>
> May the angels of mercy comfort you and bring you peace as you depart from us.
>
> May the angels of hope take you by the hand and lead you home.

All: "You will always be a part of our hearts. Go in peace."

If the group is so inclined, all join hands and sing a favorite song of the dying person or pray a familiar prayer such as the Our Father or Hail Mary.

out of the ordinary

Leaning on the Heart of God[*]

Accept the strength that comes
from the grace of Christ Jesus.

—2 Timothy 2:1

I am leaning on the heart of God.
I am resting there in silence.
All the turmoil that exhausts me
is brought to bear on this great love.

No resistance or complaint is heard
as I lean upon God's welcome.
There is gladness for my coming.
There is comfort for my pain.

I lean, and lean, and lean
upon this heart that hurts with me.
Strength lifts the weight of my distress.
Courage wraps around my troubles.

No miracle of instant recovery.
No taking away of life's burdens.
Yet, there is solace for my soul,
and refuge for my exiled tears.

It is enough for me to know
the heart of God is with me,
full of mercy and compassion,
tending to the wounds I bear.

—Joyce Rupp

[*]See *May I Have This Dance,* Joyce Rupp (Ave Maria Press) Chapter 3, March, for more on this topic.

Wounded Ones on the Road

On their way . . . talking together . . . walked by their
side . . . our own hope had been . . . they said . . . he
said . . . drew near . . . pressed him to stay . . . took the
bread . . . blessed . . . eyes opened . . .hearts burn within
. . . set out that instant. . . .

—Luke 24:13-35 (JB)

*Read the story of the two on the road to Emmaus in Luke's gospel. Listen
to their hurt and frustration. Hear what Jesus has to say to them. Go
with them to the table where they break bread with him. Pause to be
with the powerful presence of love among these three who are gathered at
table. Then proceed with the following process of reflecting on your own
woundedness.*

1. Reflect upon your own road of life. Make a list of your wounds
    or hurts. List as many as you can remember. As you look at your
    list, do the following:

    Draw a flower next to the ones that have been cared for and
    seem to be healed.

    Place a star next to the ones that seem to be partially healed.

    Place an exclamation point next to the ones that are still
    quite raw and hurtful.

2. Choose one of your wounds that has been healed. Reflect on
    how the healing happened for you. Ask this old wound to tell
    you about the wisdom you have gained from it. Offer your
    prayer of gratitude for being healed.

3. Choose one of your wounds that still needs to be healed. Ask it
    to tell you what you need in order to obtain greater healing. Pray
    to be healed of this hurt.

4. Walk with Jesus as the two did on the road to Emmaus. Talk to
    him about your life struggles, what still hurts and is in pain.

out of the ordinary

Pour out your story of woundedness to him. Let Jesus be your listening companion.

5. Go sit at the table with Jesus. Let him break bread with you. Experience the blessedness of his presence. Let him bless you and give you what you need to continue to be healed of your old wounds.

Blessing Prayer for Healing

May you* desire to be healed.

May what is wounded in your life be restored to good health.

May you be receptive to the ways in which healing needs to happen.

May you take good care of yourself.

May you extend compassion to all that hurts within your body, mind, spirit.

May you be patient with the time it takes to heal.

May you be aware of the wonders of your body, mind, and spirit and their amazing capacity to heal.

May the skills of all those who are caring for you be used to the best of their ability in returning you to good health.

May you be open to receive from those who extend kindness, care, and compassion to you.

May you rest peacefully under the sheltering wings of divine love, trusting in this gracious presence.

May you find little moments of beauty and joy to sustain you.

May you keep hope in your heart.

Hold your hands over your own heart and remember the power of love within you. Then, extend your hands of love toward the one who needs healing. Give this healing love to the one being blessed. If blessing oneself, recognize and accept this power of love within you.

—Joyce Rupp

*If praying for oneself, insert "I" instead of "you."

Easter

A Remnant of Resurrection

the time for daffodils has come.
bunches of six, ten, or twelve,
with tightly wrapped buds,
arrive from warmer lands.

like sentinels of invitation
they keep my wintered heart
leaning into Spring.

the directions say to cut
at least a half inch off the stem,
then place in water and
wait for the surprise.

behold, in the early hour of dawn,
I see resurrection on my kitchen table,
every yellowed daffodil hurrahing the morning,
stretching outward in the etched-glass vase.

but what captures my attention
is one small, thin remnant,
voluntarily discarded,
beneath the smiling daffodils.

this dry, transparent cover,
a cast-off tube of protection
once concealing a fragile bud,
conveys the price of blooming.

I pick up this remnant of resurrection
and hold it for a long, silent time,
wondering what soul-shroud of mine
needs to be unwrapped,
before I, too, am blooming.

—Joyce Rupp

A Springtime Prayer

Ever-renewing and energizing Creator,
come, stir in my dormant spiritual limbs.

Wake up my tired prayer.
Revive my weary efforts of care.
Sing hope into my discouragement.

Wash my dusty, drab attitude
with the cleansing rains of your vision.

Go deep to my roots and penetrate my faith
with the vibrancy of your grace.

Shake loose the old leftover oak leaves
of my tenacious ego-centeredness.

Coax joy to sprout from my difficulties.

Warm the buds of my relationships
so they bloom with healthy love.

Clear out my wintered debris
with the wild breeze of your liberating presence.

Nudge me, woo me, entice me, draw me to you.

I give you my trust and my gratitude
as you grace my slowly thawing spirit.

Light-filled Being, my Joy and my Hope,
let the greening in me begin!

—Joyce Rupp

Tomb-Watch

It all began with a postcard tucked inside an envelope with a letter. I'm sure my friend never knew what that small print of the fourteenth station of the cross would generate in me. Neither did I. But I did know the instant I saw the print by the southwest artist, Ettore (Ted) DeGrazia, that something (or Someone) tugged at my lenten spirit and asked me to look longer.

DeGrazia's print shows the body of Jesus wrapped in a traditional mummy-like white shroud, lying on a stone slab. Ah, but the body is not alone. All around it are shawled sorrowing angels keeping vigil. Their soft rainbow colors dare the darkness of the tomb. Slightly bowed as they sit, one knows immediately that their hearts are weary with sadness for their Beloved. They watch with a patient vigilance, attending the One who has given all. They trustfully wait for the piercing light of resurrection to banish the gloom of death's house.

I carried DeGrazia's fourteenth station with me everywhere that Lent. One day in Montana a woman stood up among the retreatants and she described how their parish has a "tomb watch" every Holy Saturday. They enter a room of physical darkness as they ponder the tomb of death and the radical eastering of Jesus. They vigil and they wait silently, as do the angels in DeGrazia's depiction of the fourteenth station.

I understood, then, the power of these angels surrounding the shrouded body of Jesus. I saw clearly how each of us needs "tomb watches" every now and then. Maybe we are keeping vigil for a part of ourselves that lies dormant and seemingly dead or lost or has fallen into a coffin of depression or despair. Maybe that shrouded figure in us is the loss of a way to pray, a deadening unforgiveness, or a body experiencing its physical limitations. Maybe our "tomb watch" is our becoming the angel of vigil, attending someone else in pain. Maybe the vigil we keep is for the people of our world as we weep for their woe or for the Earth herself as she continues to experience humanity's reckless waste and the grime of greed.

We all have our angels. They sit like DeGrazia's shawled figures who lovingly attend the shrouded body of Jesus. They now wait with us

out of the ordinary

until the light returns. And from these angels we learn how to tend the tombs of others, how to keep vigil with them in their dark dead times.

Easter is about "tomb watches." It is about love that keeps vigil and waits and believes in life, no matter how dark and empty and cold the inner space feels. Easter is about hope that is willing to sit in the tomb while it trusts in transformation. Easter is about faithful companions who keep watch with us and cheer us on as we wait for our inner resurrection.

Awaken Me

Risen One,
come, meet me
in the garden of my life.

Lure me into elation.
Revive my silent hope.
Coax my dormant dreams.
Raise up my neglected gratitude.
Entice my tired enthusiasm.
Give life to my faltering relationships.
Roll back the stone of my indifference.
Unwrap the deadness in my spiritual life.
Impart heartiness in my work.

Risen One,
send me forth as a disciple of your unwavering love,
a messenger
of your unlimited joy.

Resurrected One,
may I become
ever more convinced
that your presence lives on,
and on, and on,
and on.

Awaken me!
Awaken me!

—Joyce Rupp

Praying With the Easter Stories

Various readers could proclaim the scripture passages and all present respond with the prayers.

It may be helpful to have a small pause of reflection after each prayer.

1. So they left the tomb quickly with . . . great joy, and ran to tell his disciples (Mt 28:8).

Risen One, Bringer of Joy, plant the seeds of great gladness deep in the soil of my being. May I enjoy life, begin each day with enthusiasm, and become ever more aware of you.

2. And they (the women) came to him, took hold of his feet, and worshiped him (Mt 28:9).

Risen One, Beloved, draw me ever nearer to you. I offer you my love and devotion. I embrace you and bow to your beauty. May I commit my entire life ever more fully to you.

3. She (Mary Magdalene) went out and told those who had been with him, while they were mourning and weeping. But when they heard that he was alive and had been seen by her, they would not believe it (Mk 16:10-11).

Risen One, Truth-Bringer, open my heart to hear your voice. May I listen deeply even when tears of sorrow moisten my heart. Erase my resistance to the surprising ways you choose to enter my life.

4. They found the stone rolled away from the tomb . . . (Luke 24:2).

Risen One, Tomb-Opener, you are the power I need. Roll away the stones of unloving. Push back the rocks of discontent. Shove aside the boulders of worry. Untomb me and set me free.

5. "Why do you look for the living among the dead? He is not here, but has risen. Remember how he told you, while he was still in Galilee, that the Son of Man must be handed over to sinners, and be crucified, and on the third day rise again." Then they remembered his words . . . (Lk 24:5-8).

Risen One, Carrier of Memories, you have revealed many things to me through events and people, in the pages of scripture, and in the quiet of my heart. Carry me back in memory to savor your revelations.

6. But Peter got up and ran to the tomb; stooping and looking in, he saw the linen cloths by themselves; then he went home, amazed at what had happened (Lk 24:12).

Risen One, Source of Amazement, I run to the tomb of life, I hurry to see for myself. When I look with eyes of faith, I am amazed at what I find. That which seems dead and forsaken fills with wisdom and teachings for my life.

7. Jesus himself came near and went with them. . . . And he said to them, "What are you discussing with each other while you walk along?" (Lk 24:15-17).

Risen One, Full of Compassion, you are with me as I walk the continuing road of sorrow and joy. You listen to my longing. You fill me with the strength of your loving nearness.

8. He walked ahead as if he were going on. But they urged him strongly, saying, "Stay with us. . . ." So he went in to stay with them (Lk 24:28-29).

Risen One, Trusted Companion, I desire to be with you. Stay with me. Your presence nourishes my hunger. Your love feeds my desire for goodness. Stay with me. Stay with me.

9. Then they told what had happened on the road, and how he had been made known to them in the breaking of the bread (Lk 24:35).

Risen One, Sacred Teacher, you send me forth with blessing. You bid me tell the powerful story of your risen life. May I tell this story again and again through the witness of my life, by the quality of my love, and by the courage of my words.

10. All these were constantly devoting themselves to prayer, together with certain women, including Mary the mother of Jesus, as well as his brothers (Acts 1:14).

Risen One, Core of Community, whenever we gather, you are with us. Whenever we gather, the ancestors are near. Whenever we gather, you make of our hearts, one heart. Risen One, we welcome you into our midst.

out of the ordinary

The Easter Challenge

You believe because you can see. . . .
Happy are those who have not seen
and yet believe.

—John 20:29

Every year it happens:
earth shakes her sleepy head,
still a bit wintered and dull,
and feels new life stirring

Every year cocoons give up their treasures,
fresh shoots push through brown leaves,
seemingly dead branches shine with green,
and singing birds find their way home

Every year we hear the stories

empty tomb, surprised grievers,
runners with news and revelation,
unexpected encounters,
conversations on the road,
tales of nets filling with fish,
and breakfast on a seashore

And every year
the dull and dead in us
meets our Easter challenge:

to be open to the unexpected,
to believe beyond our security,
to welcome God in every form,
and trust in our own greening

—Joyce Rupp

Easter

Prayer to the Restorer of Entombed Vitality

Awakened One
source of inner power
restorer of tombed vitality
giver of graced gusto

you who have been raised
from the cold stone of death
come and resurrect me
from my own entombment

repair what has weakened
in my spiritual endeavors
revive my mildewed
cobwebbed relationships

lift up my waning hope
when I wail with the world's pain
restore my sense of oneness
with all of your creation

refresh my daily call
to embrace the sacred
to find you in every gesture
that dances with your heart

push back the stone
of self-centeredness
untomb my generosity
renew my dedication

raise up my dilapidated dreams
restore my ancient union
resuscitate my burning desire
re-establish my priorities
so you become the Center
of all I am and all I do

—Joyce Rupp

Come Out!

(Jn 11:43)

Jesus stood at the tomb of Lazarus,
a friend, dead, buried three days,
and he demanded, "Take the stone away!"

But Martha, sister of the dead,
turned in alarm to her friend:
"No, you can't do that. He can't come out.
He's been in there too long. He stinks!"

That fearful voice of resistance
has echoed through the ages,
leaving fragments in our souls:
"You can't find a new life.
You've been dead too long.
Don't think you can change now."

The old message repeats itself
to those life-giving parts of us
that have died and gone to stinking,
and need to be raised up:

the child in us who succumbed to neglect,
the self-esteem that was choked by fear,
the intuition that withered with mistrust,
the joy that submitted to anxiety and worry.

Many are the names of the dead in ourselves,
many are the risings that need to take place.
Jesus stands at the tomb and calls them out,
ignoring the loud protest of our inner voice
that cries: "You can't call *that* back to life!"

This Easter, welcome the inner Lazarus,
let the stone unseal the stinking.
Let the Risen Voice resurrect our deadness
and give it an entrance into light.

—Joyce Rupp

Easter

89

Slow Greening

I remember many springtimes when I'd awaken in the morning, look out the window, and zap, there this green grass would be. Robust, vibrant grass. It seemed like it was an overnight kind of thing, brown one day and bright green the next. This greening always came in the springtimes when we had drenching rains. One year, however, we had very little rain and many more cold days than usual. Each day I looked with hope, expecting to find fresh green pushing its way through the drab wintered spears of dryness. But each day I saw, instead, the same dull color before me.

When I looked closely, however, I could perceive little hints of new life and a slight changing in the color of the lawn. I could almost feel the earth straining, trying to draw forth new life from within it. I knew the green would come again, that it would just be a matter of time before warmth and moisture provided the right conditions for change and growth. Eventually, the green did return, but not until I had waited a long time for rain to come and drench the land.

This process of the earth's greening after a long winter reminds me of our spiritual "eastering," the inner transformation and rebirthing that comes after we've had a long winter spell of the spirit. The dead, brown grass is there for eons in our hearts, or so it seems. No amount of hurry, or push, or desire can make the green happen any sooner.

I think of people I know who are longing for an inner greening, and are yet in the throes of a spiritual winter: a widow whose husband recently died at a much too early age; a man who is struggling with a new career in midlife and fears his ability to cope with the challenges it requires; the friend whose husband has applied for work far from home and the painful questions it leaves her about what she will do with her own career and friends; a colleague who fell into deep, clinical depression and struggles to live through each day with meager energy. Each one needs an "eastering," a bright greening, and oh, how they long for it to come soon.

But it may be a painstakingly slow process, a tiny bit of life gradually weaving through the pain and questions. Eastering isn't always a quick step out of the tomb. Sometimes rising from the dead takes a long, slowly-greening time. It can't be hurried.

It is my hope for you this Easter season that you will trust the resurrection of your spirit, believe that joy and new life will come for you, even though it may not be there for you now. If you are one of the fortunate ones whose soul sings with happy alleluias this Easter, may you turn often to those who are still awaiting their greening and walk hopefully with them.

Risen One, open our minds and hearts. Let us see and welcome your presence.

1. Then their eyes were opened, and they recognized him (Lk 24:31).

All around me Easter is happening. God continues to reveal love, to extend invitations to growth, to offer me hope. What is God's latest revelation to me? How has this changed my life?

2. Jesus said to them, "Come and have breakfast" (Jn 21:12).

Jesus invited the disciples to come and to be nourished with food that he had prepared. What food am I being offered for the nourishment of my spirit? What food do I accept and what do I reject?

3. "He is going ahead of you to Galilee; there you will see him" (Mt 28:7).

Galilee . . . the place of much action and healing during the ministry of Jesus. I have my own Galilee. It is there that I will see the Risen One. Is there anything I need to change or adapt so that I will more readily recognize the Holy One in my life?

4. "Do not be afraid; I know that you are looking for Jesus who was crucified. He is not here; for he has been raised . . ." (Mt 28:5-6).

Fear filled the hearts of those who had loved Jesus. They found it difficult to believe the Easter message. What keeps me from hearing the truth that is being offered to me? What is my resistance?

5. "Blessed are those who have not seen and yet have come to believe" (Jn 20:29).

Jesus chided Thomas for his lack of faith. When all the evidence is not yet in, is it difficult for me to believe in God's movement in my life? How adept am I at living with mystery?

6. Jesus said to her, "Mary!" (Jn 20:16).

In the moment of hearing her name called, Mary recognized Jesus. With the sound of her name, she was bonded in love once again. When and how have I known intimacy with the Holy One? Do I believe that I, too, am very dear in God's eyes?

out of the ordinary

7. "Were not our hearts burning within us while he was talking to us on the road, while he was opening the scriptures to us?" (Lk 24:32).

What a wonderful moment of surprise and joy for the two on the road to Emmaus. They must have felt amazing relief after their intense struggle. I, too, have had my life events that were blessed with joy and happiness. For what do I offer gratitude this day?

8. "Why do you look for the living among the dead?" (Lk 24:5).

The question asked by the messenger of God to those who peered into the empty tomb can also be my question. I may also be looking for life in the wrong places, in old issues or things of the past which I need to let go. Where am I looking for life?

9. So they left the tomb quickly with fear and great joy, and ran to tell his disciples (Mt 28:8).

The women went to tell the good news. They ran with excitement and joy and a bit of trepidation too. How do I proclaim, through my life and words, that I am aware of the powerful presence of God in my midst? How do I witness to what I believe?

10. Jesus himself stood among them and said to them, "Peace be with you" (Lk 24:36).

As Jesus came among them he recognized the fear and disbelief that filled his followers' hearts. He greeted them with "Peace." How will I greet myself and my world with peace during the Easter season?

Reflection on Luke 24:13-35

Where have you been on the road to Emmaus? Where are you now?

Heading back

Discouraged, hopes dashed, disheartened . . .
What is your main emotional response to life?

Telling your story

Sorting out what is going on, looking at expectations and the reality
of life . . .
How do you stay in touch with your story?

Listening to the connections

Discovering truths, seeing the deeper realities . . .
How do you see your life in relation to the journey of death and
resurrection?

Pressed him to stay on

Desire for God, moments of intimacy in solitude and community . . .
How and when do you invite God into your life?

Recognition and hearts set afire

Events, people, inner awareness that have restored the fire in your
heart . . .
When was the last time that you felt "enkindled" in your relationship
with God?

Set out to tell

A ministry alive with a relationship with the Beloved, a service
shared with others that is energized by daily encounters with this
Beloved . . .
What do you most want to "go and tell" to the people who are in
your life?

Now in your life

Which of the steps in the Emmaus story is most active in your own
life story at the present time?

out of the ordinary

Epiphany

The Song of the Stars

stars twinkle, shine, illuminate,
fill a black night with radiance,
guide strangers with their glow,
bless a sad heart with brightness.

but do the stars also sing?
can you hear their music
as they dance with brilliance
on a dark December night?

if you listen closely,
you can catch their melodies
across the ancient sky:
chants, hymns, ballads,
lullabies, and symphonies,

stars sailing across the cosmos,
humming their radiant tunes,
silver notes sent on angel wings,
received in open, loving hearts.

shepherds on hillside were ready,
and, oh, the melodies they heard.
the glory and surprise of good news
sang and danced around their heads.

three travelers heard a secret tune,
a guiding star urging them to follow,
a lilting song of mystery and journey,
of bearing gifts from fields afar.

these same stars sang at our birthing,
enticing songs within our soul.
their ancient music stirs us deeply,
if we learn to listen well.

—Joyce Rupp

out of the ordinary

The Gift

(a guided visualization)

Find a quiet spot to be alone.

Sit with your back straight, feet on the floor.

Begin with taking some deep breaths and letting them out slowly.

Ask the Spirit of God to open your being, to quiet you. . . .

Picture the scene of the Three Wise Ones coming to offer homage
and gifts to Jesus, the One sent by God. . . .

See yourself as one of the Wise Ones. . . .

You are coming to offer a gift. . . .

There is a wonderfully wrapped gift in your hands. . . .

Inside the gift are aspects and qualities of your life that you most
enjoy and appreciate. Reflect upon these aspects and qualities:

> Which ones are especially significant for you?

> Which ones have been most apparent during the past year?

> Which ones have seemed hidden or absent during the past year?

Now gather these qualities of your life into your gift.

Visualize yourself coming and presenting your gift-wrapped package. . . .

As you offer this gift of yourself, see the love, joy, delight with which
your gift is received. . . .

Visualize a gift being offered to you. It, too, is beautifully wrapped.

It has a note-card on it, a special message from Jesus to you.

Imagine what is written on the note-card. . . .

Receive the gift, open it, and ponder its significance for your life. . . .

After you have received the gift, offer thanks to the Holy One for
this gift in whatever way seems best for you. . . .

Complete your time of prayer by writing down your thoughts and
feelings, and a prayer to the Holy One who gifts you in this new
year.

The Seeker

I do not ride on camels
through a wind-swept desert.
I do not carry gifts
that are fit for a king.
I do not see the star
that guides the stalwart riders.

Yet I, too, am seeking.
I, too, am longing.
I go among the busy days
yearning for the Unknown One.

In the breath of a prayer,
in the care of a friend,
in the beauty of a bird,
a star-like glimpse comes to me.

A flicker of hope arises,
enough to stay in the fray,
to keep searching for the One
who is slowly revealed
in tiny sparks of daily encounters.

Holy One, you who reveal,
make manifest your presence.
Open the eyes of my heart.
Awaken my unattuned spirit.

Bring me to full attention,
so that I come to know,
in my every moment,
your radiant star of guidance.

—Joyce Rupp

out of the ordinary

Epiphany

(Matthew 2:1-12)

they listened deep inside,
far into the darkness
where even a tiny bit of light
seemed like sunburst in the heart.

they pondered the silent music
that echoed in their prayer:
"Go. Search. Look. Follow. Find."

a journey without precedent,
adventure wrought with risk,
a time of travel filled with faith.

they went lovingly, eagerly,
into the night of their lives,
trusting they would find the way.

they paused to inquire, to study,
they went on in faith, patiently,
following with the hearts' eye,

and "the sight of the star
filled them with delight."

a journey not in vain,
a patient search rewarded,
their steady courage in the unknown
led them to their heart's delight.

they found the long-sought One,
waiting to be found,
longing to be discovered,
as they traveled the far stretches
of their long and hidden night.

—Joyce Rupp

A Prayer for Epiphany

On entering the house, they saw the child with Mary his
mother; and they knelt down and paid him homage.
Then, opening their treasure chests, they offered him
gifts of gold, frankincense, and myrrh.

—Matthew 2:11

Radiant One, every day is an epiphany in which I, too, can pay you
homage. Every day I can kneel before you and open the treasure chest
of my life. In there, I find unending gifts of every kind to offer you.
Every day I bring my gratitude for you, my desire to grow more loving, my longing to be true. Every day I reach into that treasure chest
and offer my trust that you are near, my hope for all you promise, my
belief in what is unseen. Every day I offer my desire to live justly, my
commitment to be generous, my struggle to be whole.

Divine Light, I give these gifts and so much more. The treasure chest
is boundless. Each time I reach within I see you smiling at my gesture,
for you, great Giver of Gifts, have placed each treasure there. You greet
my gift with welcoming pleasure when it returns back home to you.

Bestower of Gifts, thank you for all that my treasure chest of life
holds. I will look daily for my persistent star of recognition. May it
stand boldly over the house of my heart where you dwell, so that I will
be aware of your presence and pause to give you homage.

Justice

Apology to My Brothers and Sisters in Developing Countries

To my brothers and sisters in developing countries:

While I was deciding which oat bran cereal to eat this morning, you were searching the ground for leftover grains from the passing wheat truck.

While I was jogging at the health center, you were working in the wealthy landowner's field under a scorching sun.

While I was choosing between diet and regular soda, your parched lips were yearning for a sip of clean water.

While I complained about the poor service in the gourmet restaurant, you were gratefully eating a bowl of rice.

While I poured my "fresh and better" detergent into the washing machine, you stood in the river with your bundle of clothes.

While I watched the evening news on my wide-screen television set, you were being terrorized and taunted by a dictatorial government.

While I read the newspaper and drank my cup of steaming coffee, you walked the long, dusty miles to a crowded schoolroom to learn how to read.

While I scanned the ads for a bargain on an extra piece of clothing, you woke up and put on the same shirt and pants that you have worn for many months.

While I built a fourteen-room house for the three of us, your family of ten found shelter in a one-room hut.

While I went to church last Sunday and felt more than slightly bored, you stood on the land with those around you and felt gratitude to God for being alive for one more day.

My brothers and sisters, forgive me for my arrogance and my indifference. Forgive me for my greed of always wanting newer, bigger, and better things. Forgive me for not doing my part to change the unjust systems that keep you suffering and impoverished. I offer you my promise to become more aware of your situation and to change my lifestyle as I work for the transformation of our world.

The Blessing of Compassion

Compassion holds both beauty and challenge. It is based on the belief that we are united with all beings. Their joy and sorrow is our joy and sorrow because of this deep and intimate connection. To be truly compassionate means to approach another with the nonjudgment and the unconditional love that Jesus had when he met those who were suffering.

This prayer can be used with groups; the blessing is done in pairs with the two people facing each other. They both touch the other's forehead, ears, etc., while the leader says the words of the blessing. For the last section, the group is invited to repeat the words after the leader, whispering them in the other person's ear.

The prayer can also be used by one person blessing another while praying the prayers. It is essential when this prayer is used to ask the one being blessed if he or she is comfortable with someone touching his or her eyes, ears, etc. If he or she is not, then the one offering the blessing can simply hold a hand near that particular part of the body as the blessing is being prayed.

1. Touching the forehead

May you approach all other beings with Christ-like compassion, observing them with kindness. May you let go of all harsh judgments.

2. Touching the ears

May you be aware of the suffering of those around you, and of all those in the cosmos. May your ears be open to hear their cries of distress.

3. Touching the mouth

May you have the courage and wisdom to speak up for those who are wronged, to be a voice for those who suffer from injustice of any form.

4. Touching the hands

May you be open to receive from others when you are in need. May you be ready to give when someone needs to receive your gifts.

5. Touching the heart

May you be willing to meet your own suffering. May you do so with deep compassion for yourself.

6. Touching the feet

May your faith give you strength when you stand beneath the cross of another.

7. Embracing (hugging) the other person *(whisper in his or her ear)*

May you always know the shelter of God when you are hurting and in pain. May you trust this Compassionate Being to protect you and to comfort you. May you be at peace.

A Prayer of Compassion

This prayer is based on each of the seven sorrows of Mary. The following response can be said or sung. *

Mater Dolorosa, Mother of Sorrows, you know our pain.

1. The Prophecy of Simeon (Lk 2:27-35)

We unite with those who are stunned, shocked, dismayed, distraught over distressful news that will bring suffering to them in the future. . . .

2. The Flight Into Egypt (Mt 2:13-15)

We unite with those who are in dangerous situations, those who need to flee from harm. . . .

3. The Loss of the Child Jesus in the Temple (Lk 2:43-51)

We unite with those who are searching frantically for loved ones or for some part of their life that they need to discover. . . .

4. Mary Meets Jesus Carrying His Cross (Lk 23:27)

We unite with ourselves, with the pain and hurt that we meet when we enter into our own life situations. . . .

5. Mary Stands Beneath the Cross (Jn 19:25-27)

We unite with those who vigil beneath the cross of another, unable to take the pain away from those they love. . . .

6. Mary Receives the Dead Body of Jesus in Her Arms (Jn 19:38)

We unite with those who are receiving loss and death into the arms of their lives. . . .

7. Jesus Is Placed in the Tomb (Jn 19:39-42)

We unite with those who are saying farewell to those they love. We join with all who need to let go and move on with their lives.

*Refer to the Appendix—Chants

Litany of Remembrance

I remember the children of the world. As Jesus called to the children to come to him, so I gather in prayer the children of my world who are hurting. I embrace them with loving kindness and with a desire to mend the systems that bring such pain to their young lives. I remember the children:

. . . who will go hungry today,

. . . whose parents are on drugs,

. . . who have no one to teach them to read,

. . . who are handicapped and unattended,

. . . who do not know love,

. . . who live in filth and degradation,

. . . who have no friends,

. . . who are not listened to,

. . . who have never been sung to or read to or taken by the hand or experienced earth's mystery and beauty,

. . . who do not have anyone to tuck them into bed at night,

. . . who are shunned or mistreated because of their color, their religion, or the place where they live,

. . . who have no awareness of their inner goodness,

. . . who have stopped believing in love,

. . . who are filled with anger and hate,

. . . who are receiving a poor education,

. . . who are ill or in pain,

. . . who are grieving the death of a loved one,

. . . who are suffering from AIDS or drug-related diseases,

. . . who feel lonely, desolate, and unloved,

. . . who are filled with fear for their lives,

. . . who hear only harsh words and hostile language,

. . . who have been bruised, beaten, and mutilated,

. . . who are victims of incest, rape, and pornography,

. . . who hide in fear from the sounds of war,

. . . who are ill and have no medical attention.

Yes, I pray for the children of my world today and I pray for each man and woman of this world, including myself, that we will do our part to create better living conditions for these children. Show us the way and prod us into action, God of justice and compassion!

We Are One

*Place a large globe on a stand in the center of the group. In each of the four directions, place various colored cloths and items that are symbolic of people who dwell in each of the four directions of the Earth. For the voices: various readers alternate as the voice of the people. All readers proclaim the last line together: "We are one." The whole group then repeats after them: "We are one." ***

In the tradition of our Native American sisters and brothers, we address the four directions of the Earth, remembering how the Spirit of God resides there and how all of us are united as one.

East

All face the east (place silken cloths, Buddhist bell or gong).

I am the people of the East.

I am the Chinese merchant.

I am the veiled woman of Iran.

I am the Vietnamese fishing family.

I am the Tibetan Buddhist nun.

I am the office worker biking in crowded streets.

I am the herder of reindeer in Lapland.

I am the forgotten one on the streets of Calcutta.

I am the mountain climber of the Himalayas.

I am your sister.

I am your brother.

We are one.

Prayer

This prayer follows after the voices of each direction.

Creator of All, we join our minds and hearts with the people of our planet Earth. We recognize the deep bond that we have with each created being. We rejoice in your sacred presence among us and within us. Divine Oneness, we celebrate the goodness, the beauty, the talents, and the spirituality of all these brothers and sisters of ours. We stand in solidarity with all those who suffer in any way. Rekindle our love, revitalize our compassion, and renew our awareness of the unity we share with all beings.

South

All face the south (place woven fabrics of bright colors, rattles).

I am the people of the South.

I am the weavers of colorful cloth in South America.

I am the singers and dancers of Haiti.

I am the surviving bush-people of the Kalahari desert.

I am the factory worker in Mexico.

I am the mother of the disappeared in Central America.

I am the orphanage director in Africa.

I am the village shaman in the South Pacific Islands.

I am the aboriginal children playing in Australia.

I am your sister.

I am your brother.

We are one.

Prayer

(as above)

West

All face the west (place cottons and denim, flute).

I am the people of the West.

I am the sheepherders of the Alps.

I am the forest ranger in the Rockies.

I am the winemaker in the Mediterranean.

I am the housewife in Poland.

I am the rancher in unfenced lands.

I am the widow in Bosnia.

I am the child in a high-rise apartment.

I am the nurse practioner in a clinic.

I am the peacekeepers in war-torn lands.

I am your sister.

I am your brother.

We are one.

Prayer

(as above)

North

All face the north (place furs or other warm material, drums).

I am the people of the North.

I am the children of the Ojibway tribe.

I am the Inuit fishing in glacial waters.

I am the teacher in Vancouver.

I am the European immigrant.

I am the Huron native organizing for justice.

I am the grandmother in Nova Scotia.

I am the farmer on the Canadian prairie.

I am the oil worker of Alaska.

I am the waitress in a rural cafe.

I am your sister.

I am your brother.

We are one.

Prayer

(as above)

* As an adaptation of this ritual, after the voices of one direction have been proclaimed, there could be a pause and those present could add other voices that
come to mind for that particular direction. Also, a song that is representative of
that direction could also be sung; or the refrain from a song that speaks to our
oneness with all beings could be sung at the close of each direction.

out of the ordinary

Prayer for Awareness

Generous God, you smile upon the wide diversity and beauty in the humanity whom you have created, but you weep at the great divide between the rich and the poor. I come today with the taste of ego-centeredness on my spiritual breath. I beg to have greater awareness and a deeper commitment to what will heal my world. Help me to make good decisions about my daily living so that who I am and what I do can have a positive effect on my brothers and sisters everywhere on this vast planet.

Stretch my vision so that I do not forget those who hunger and search for shelter each day. Remind me when I am using and buying material things, to do so with care. Enable me to use the Earth's resources responsibly so that there will be enough to go around for all who live on this green planet today and in the future.

Awaken me each day to gratitude for all that I so easily take for granted. Let my eyes do more than just read the stories in the daily paper or watch them on the evening news. Let my eyes take those stories to my heart where I am one with all who dwell on the Earth. Touch my compassion so that I know the pain of the hungry, the violated, the homeless, the burdened, and all those who yearn for some of my riches.

Compassionate Creator, stir in my soul. Call to me again and again, to be a true child of the universe. May I be attentive and alert to how you would have me live my abundant life. Grant me the generosity to share it with others.

Lent

The Echo of Ashes

"Remember you are dust
and to dust you shall return."

the large brown bowl
rests on a purple cloth
its roundness holding ashes
freshly burned
black and ready for wearing.

blackened thumbs
press the ancient sign
upon the waiting foreheads.

I hear the message repeated
until it haunts and hunts me down:
remember, remember, remember
you are dust, dust, only dust
someday only dust will remain.

the echo of the Lent-stained ashes
speaks the truth of my humanity:
the humbleness of my beginning,
the simplicity of my departure.

A few wise words
echoing through Ash Wednesday
urge me to deeper things:
renewed dedication,
constant compassion,
and mindful awareness.

I leave marveling
at how simple and sublime
is this envelope of the soul,
which one day returns
to dust, dust, only dust.

—Joyce Rupp

out of the ordinary

Create in Me a Clean Heart

Create in me a clean heart, O God,
and put a new and right spirit within me.

—Psalm 51:10

† *Create in me a clean heart*, open and receptive, so that I may embrace the many ways you choose to visit my life.

† *Create in me a clean heart*, cleared of the refuse of old battles with others and deadly opposition with myself.

† *Create in me a clean heart*, purified through the daily disruptions and the life encounters that take me beyond my grasping control and ego-centeredness.

† *Create in me a clean heart*, freed from the clutter of cultural enticements, so that I can enjoy the beauty of life's simple things and relish the gifts I easily take for granted.

† *Create in me a clean heart*, bathed from harsh thoughts, shame, and perfectionistic tendencies, warmly welcoming others with the embrace of nonjudgment.

† *Create in me a clean heart*, brushed free of frantic busyness, so that I will have time to dwell with you in the listening space of solitude and silence.

† *Create in me a clean heart*, rinsed of the residue of false messages about my identity, enabling my inner goodness and light to shine through all I am and do.

† *Create in me a clean heart*, cleansed of anxiety and lack of trust, restoring in me an enduring faith in your abiding presence and unconditional love.

† *Create in me a clean heart*, scrubbed of racism and prejudice, drawing me toward all as my sisters and brothers.

† *Create in me a clean heart*, washed with your mercy and strengthened by your love, helping me move beyond whatever keeps me from union with you.

Create a clean heart in me, God. Dust off the unmindful activity that constantly collects there. De-clutter my heart from harsh judgments and negativity. Wash away my resistance to working through difficult relationships. Rinse off my un-loving so the beauty of my generous and kind heart can shine forth. Remove whatever keeps me from following in your compassionate footsteps. Amen.

Carrying the Cross

Response: Jesus, grant us strength to carry our cross.

† On those days when life seems too demanding with all its cares, burdens, and concerns . . .

† When we experience great loneliness deep inside and the pain of separation fills our spirits . . .

† When we feel the pain of our world and unite in compassion with the Earth's suffering people . . .

† When we struggle with decision-making and the time comes to make good choices about our lives . . .

† When we are with others in their physical pain or when we vigil with one who has a terminal illness . . .

† When we are asked to go the extra mile, to be generous with our time and our presence . . .

† When we feel weary and worn out, when it seems like all of our energy has been drained away . . .

† When we are challenged to risk our security and to accept new growth in our relationship with you . . .

† When we experience the effects of aging or extended illness on our bodies or our minds . . .

† When we feel discouraged, desolate, and depressed and want to withdraw from others . . .

† When worries and concerns choke our peacefulness and leave us with anxiety and fear . . .

† When we harbor old wounds and are called to offer or to receive forgiveness . . .

Together

Crucified Jesus, help us to take up our cross day by day. Through these crosses we can grow closer to you. Help us to lean on you and to learn from you. May we not give in to self-pity or self-doubt. Rather, let us trust in your presence which strengthens us. Encourage us on our tomb-like days. Remind us of your resurrection. Help us to keep our vision focused on life and growth. Amen.

A Lenten Reflection

I was standing in an aisle in the grocery store when a sharp spiritual pain pinched my awareness and let me see the rest of the world. I was appalled. I realized I could buy anything in the store that I wanted. The richness of my life slapped me in the face as I stood there, thinking about how many people do not even have a store like that available to them, let alone the money to purchase what is in it.

Not long after that experience, I read some statistics in an article by Joan Chittister that increased my awareness of my own richness in light of the world's poverty:

> Social statisticians tell us that if the earth's population were a village of 100 people, there would be 57 Asians, 21 Europeans, and 8 Africans. Only 14 people in the village would be from both North and South America combined. Seventy of the people in this village would be nonwhite. Seventy would be non-Christian. Seventy would be illiterate. Fifty of them would be malnourished. Fifty percent of all the money in the village would be held by six people—and all of them would be white, male Americans. . . . *

Reading *Angela's Ashes* by Frank McCourt increased my awareness of how fifty percent of the world are impoverished while I sit in my comfortable shelter, feasting daily on good food. As McCourt described going hungry day after day in his memoir of a childhood in Ireland's desolate time, I thought of how rarely I consider the rest of humanity, while day after day I am in my snug, smug little world of satisfaction.

My awareness continued to deepen as I read McCourt's description of the three small boys sleeping on one old, raggedy coat, covered by two thin ones in the damp, cold climate, and of his licking the newspapers he found in which someone's fish and chips had been wrapped. This is not just something that has happened in the past. This kind of situation continues to exist, day after day, in many cities, villages, and isolated country places.

But there is also hope. There are people in wealthy nations whose awareness of the rest of the world is making a difference. They want

out of the ordinary

to help. They are working to change the great gap between the haves and have-nots. I see the choices these generous and compassionate people are making. Their selflessness and kind-heartedness encourages me to make better decisions about how I live and how I give. I do not believe that it is a matter of condemning a comfortable life but, rather, of wanting this for all people. It is good that we are challenged to use our resources in such a way that others can also have a more humane life. It is essential that we are reminded often that each human being is our sister or our brother. It is the message that Jesus taught so long ago. It is an ageless teaching and we are always in need of re-learning and living the message. Lent is a good time to re-enter the heart of this teaching.

*National Catholic Reporter, February 20, 1998.

Clothed With the Qualities of Christ

The desire to focus on Lent as a time of being "clothed with love" leapt in me one evening at a gathering for Celtic studies. That night two of our members led us in a ceremony to honor the feast of Brigid (Feb. 1). They told stories about the legend of Brigid and how the Celts celebrated the protective, curative powers of her mantle. The Celts would take a cloth at sunset on her feast and place it outside their home. That night Brigid would hear their prayers and bring healing and protection for all in the house. They kept this cloth in the home until the next year's feast.

Then we were each given a small lace cloth as a "mantle of Brigid" and asked to reflect on what protective and healing powers we needed in our lives. I felt myself needing to be clothed with loving-kindness. As the ceremony was nearing completion, the scripture from Colossians suddenly came to my mind. I took my "mantle of loving kindness" home with me that night and it became my lenten practice that year.

> Clothe yourselves with compassion, kindness, humility, meekness, and patience. Bear with one another and, if anyone has a complaint against another, forgive each other. . . . Above all, clothe yourselves with love, which binds everything together in perfect harmony.
>
> —Colossians 3:12-14

Jesus, Mentor and Friend, your life and ministry were constantly clothed with love.

I hold the image of your loving qualities and virtues close to me as I pray:

When my spiritual clothes are soiled with negativity and neglect, may I have the desire and energy to clean them.

When my spiritual clothes droop, sag, and do not fit, may I have the wisdom and determination to let my words and actions fit my values and beliefs.

When my spiritual clothes need changing, may I have the ability to make good decisions and the courage to follow through with the necessary changes.

When my spiritual clothes are torn and need mending, may I make amends and be open to forgiveness and reconciliation.

When my spiritual clothes are not accepted by others, may I have the self-affirmation to be my true self and not give in to the demands of others.

When my spiritual clothes become thin and frayed, may I strengthen them with a garment of loving-kindness.

Jesus, transform all I am and all I do into the kind of love that permeated your presence. Clothe me with your love and grant me grace to be truly kind and caring. May my spiritual clothes be spun from the gold of your goodness and last into eternity.

I Must Stay at Your House Today

[Zacchaeus] was trying to see who Jesus was, but on account of the crowd he could not, because he was short in stature. So he ran ahead and climbed a sycamore tree to see him. . . . When Jesus came to the place, he looked up and said to him, "Zacchaeus, hurry and come down; for I must stay at your house today." So he hurried down and was happy to welcome him.

—Luke 19:3-6

Jesus, this Lent I am yearning to wear a Zacchaeus heart.
I am wanting to hear you call my name just as you did his.
I am anxious to know that you are inviting yourself to my home.
I am humbled, amazed, excited, and astounded, just as he was.

But that is where the desire to wear a Zacchaeus heart stops,
because I know what happens when you visit someone's house.
Conversations occur. Choices are presented. Changes happen.
That's because you look for more than dust when you come to visit
and you talk about things more vital than the weather.
You move into the heart's dimension. You gaze deeply.
You don't just dwell. You interact. You activate.
You dwell so lovingly that the truth cannot be resisted.

This Lent help me to welcome you and yearn for your love.
Grant me a Zacchaeus heart that turns around and sees the truth.
I need the gaze of your love to remind me of my truest self.
I, too, need the strong call to make amends and start anew.
Hurry, Jesus, come and stay at my house today.

—Joyce Rupp

out of the ordinary

The Farewell Tear

a feast of friendship
a story of betrayal
a memory of gifts given

you look with such intense love
on each one gathered there,
mist covers your deep brown eyes
as you hold each one in your gaze,
you close your eyes and I see
the farewell tear of friendship
as it follows the curve of your cheek.

you take the bread,
bless it gently, profoundly,
with old words and new.
(do you mean to say it is yourself?)

and then the wine,
again with words old and new.
(do you meant to say this, too,
is now yourself?)

you look again at each one there
and give the eternal gift:
"remember me and do the same."

like those around the table then,
so with us who gather now,
if we knew how close our hearts
are held inside of yours,
we would always be amazed
that you meant this for us, too.

how shall we ever be brave enough
to do what you have done,
when grief engulfs our every breath
and each memorial word
is laden with our loss?

—Joyce Rupp

Lent

Mary

Feast of the Annunciation

(Luke 1:26-38)

Leader

We rejoice in the call and response of Mary, woman of faith. We celebrate the power of the Divine Presence in the many forms in which God comes to us. As we join in gratitude for the faith of Mary, Servant of the Holy One, we pray to renew our commitment to this Unending Love. We now offer the following prayers to the One who unceasingly woos us into deeper faith:

The following could be prayed by alternate sides or alternate readers.

1. Spirit of love, linger long at the door of our hearts. Call to us time and again until we hear your voice and respond to you.

2. Teach us to listen for you in every corner of our lives and to await your messengers in the most unexpected situations and conditions.

3. Open our minds and our hearts so that we will respond as your servant Mary did. Help us to give our "yes" to you even though our faith groans and wobbles with doubts and concerns.

4. Encourage us to recognize our fears when they rise up. Give us the strength we need. Let us not give in to anxious trepidations when they bombard us with negativity.

5. Keep nudging us to move toward growth when our resistance holds us back. When we question the impracticality or the seeming impossibility of these nudges, give us wisdom and courage to let go of what restrains us.

6. Still and quiet our souls. May we hear the whisper of your divine call, asking us each day to accept the treasure of your life within us.

7. May the music of Mary's own trustful response sing in our spirits. Gift us with the ability to move forward into the unknown, confident that you will guide and direct us.

All

Mary, thank you for your attentive receptivity. We, too, are not alone in the call to face an unknown future. May we trust that the Holy One will shelter us and accompany us on our spiritual journey. May the spirit of your child, Jesus, live on in us. May we, too, be men and women of great love, carrying the Divine Presence in the womb of our hearts.

As a closing to this prayer, the following chant could be sung.*

My Soul Rejoices

My soul rejoices in my God

My soul rejoices in my God

The God of justice,

The God of mercy,

The God of compassion.

*See Appendix—Chants

Mary

The Visitation

Mary, you went hurriedly over hillsides,
many of them, to be with aunt Elizabeth,
whose womb also swelled with surprise

You, the woman of youth and vigor,
weary from the long road's rigors,
wondering still about the mystery within

Elizabeth, wrinkled and wise,
weary from the child kicking inside,
(already a hint of wildness in him)

The two of you, meeting at the door,
weeping and laughing at the same time,
each one gasping at the other's fertility

And leaping between and among you,
those two frisky fetuses, yet to be born,
the prophet and the One to be proclaimed

Did they feel the love of your hospitality?
Did they swim and sway with your voice?
Did they listen with tiny, eager ears to all

that passed between the two of you
in the days and weeks that swiftly passed,
growing and feeding on your rich love?

I don't know which I'd have wanted more,
to be in one of those glorious filled wombs
or in the house of that woman-blessed place

—Joyce Rupp

Mary, Mother of Sorrows*

Leader

We gather in honor of Mary, mentor and model of faith. We remember the sorrows which shaped her world. We celebrate her gift of compassion. We join with her as we pray for all those who experience difficulties in their lives.

The First Sorrow: The Prophecy of Simeon (Lk 2:27-35)

Reader

Within a moment of joy, devastating announcement,
the heart shudders with fear, trembling as the future unfolds.

Pause for reflection on Mary's response to Simeon's prophecy.

All

Compassionate God,
there are many people in our world today
who are hearing difficult news.
They will need an anchor of strength
to keep them from being swept away
in their waves of worry and fear.
You can be this anchor of strength for them.
In particular, we pray for . . . (*pause for silent or vocal remembering*).
Mary, teach us how to be people of faith.

Sing: Mater Dolorosa, Mother of Sorrows, you know our pain.**

The Second Sorrow: The Flight Into Egypt (Mt 2:13-15)

Reader

A dream taps on the inner world, warning of danger and death.
two frightened parents hurry to find refuge for their beloved child.

Pause to reflect on what Mary experienced as they fled to Egypt.

All

Loving Shelter,
there are many people in our world

Mary

129

who live in dangerous or hurtful situations.
They need courage to leave what is harmful.
They need safety and protection.
You can be the peace they seek.
You can be the shelter they need
as they make decisions and move on with their lives.
In particular, we pray for . . . (*pause for silent or vocal remembering*).
Mary, teach us how to be people of faith.

Sing: Mater Dolorosa, Mother of Sorrows, you know our pain.

The Third Sorrow: Loss of the Child Jesus in the Temple
(Lk 2:43-51)

Reader

Frantic footsteps hasten back, retracing roads recently traveled.
A mother presses on in her search, finding a child whose wisdom
takes her deeper into mystery.

Pause to reflect on how Mary felt when she lost her son and when she found him.

All

God of the lonely and troubled,
there are many people in my world
who are searching for something or someone they treasure.
There are parents filled with heartache for their lost child.
There are distressed people searching for themselves.
There are countless grieving ones who are looking
for a part of their life that once gave them happiness.
Bless all who are searching for their lost treasure, especially . . .
(*pause for silent or vocal remembering*).
May they turn to you often and draw comfort from your guiding
presence.
Mary, teach us how to be people of faith.

Sing: Mater Dolorosa, Mother of Sorrows, you know our pain.

The Fourth Sorrow: Mary Meets Jesus Carrying His Cross
(Lk 23:27)

Reader

Mother and son, face to face, suffering in each one's heart.
We meet the pain in our life, embracing it with kindness.

Pause to reflect on what stirred within Mary when she met Jesus on the way to his death.

All

Enduring Love,
when we are experiencing troubled times
help us to be attentive to our own spirit.
We need to believe that our heartaches
are also worthy of a compassionate gaze.
Teach us how to offer kindness
to the part of us that is in pain.
With your grace we can overcome
any obstacle that keeps us
from tending to our own needs.
Remembering your great love,
we turn toward ourselves with compassion
and reach out with tenderness
as we lovingly embrace the hurting part of our self.
We remember those who need to offer compassion to their own
wounds . . . (*pause for silent or vocal remembering*).
Mary, teach us how to be people of faith.

Sing: Mater Dolorosa, Mother of Sorrows, you know our pain.

The Fifth Sorrow: Mary Stands Beneath the Cross
(Jn 19:25-27)

Reader

A mother waits while her son dies, unable to hold, to touch, to comfort; standing, vigiling, entering his agony. How much can a mother endure?

Pause to reflect on the endurance of Mary as she stood beneath the cross.

Mary

131

All

Crucified One,
may all who hang upon a cross
of suffering and sorrow,
or stand beneath a cross today,
find comfort and consolation
in your abiding presence.
Ease their pain and suffering.
Free them from discouragement.
Gentle their harsh emotions.
Cease their restlessness.
Coax them away from despair.
We especially remember those who hang upon a cross today . . .
(*pause for silent or vocal remembering*).
Mary, teach us how to be people of faith.

Sing: Mater Dolorosa, Mother of Sorrows, you know our pain.

The Sixth Sorrow: Mary Receives the Dead Body of Jesus
(Jn 19:38)

Reader

A mother's generous lap, holding what remains of a son,
receiving him as lovingly in death as she first held him, wet from the
womb.

Pause to reflect on Mary's receiving Jesus from the cross.

All

God of the desolate,
give your strength and courage
to all suffering ones,
especially those who feel
the ache of a deep loss today.
Gently open their hearts
and increase their capacity
to be with their great hurt.
Help them to be a living Pietà
of kindness and tenderness.
Draw them into your heart

out of the ordinary

so that your deep and strong love
will resound in their experience.
We remember today those who are experiencing a significant loss . . .
(*pause for silent or vocal remembering*).
Mary, teach us how to be people of faith.

Sing: Mater Dolorosa, Mother of Sorrows, you know our pain.

The Seventh Sorrow: Jesus Is Laid in the Tomb (Jn 19:39-42)

Reader

A kind-hearted child is laid to rest and a loving mother bids him
farewell.
She walks away with mystery in her heart and a thousand tears in
her grieving soul.

Pause to reflect on Mary's grief as Jesus is laid in the tomb.

All

Mary, you have been there before us.
You have stood at the tomb of farewell.
We, too, often face painful endings.
Like you, we need to eventually let go,
believing that the Holy One will console us.
You know how grief engulfs the heart
and tries to strangle the hope it contains.
You have felt the drain of a great loss
and the emptiness it creates inside.
Teach us how to have confidence in God
when we question what the future holds.
Strengthen our faith as we try to let go
of whatever keeps us from growing deeper.
We remember those who are moving through painful farewells . . .
(*pause for silent or vocal remembering*).
Mary, teach us how to be people of faith.

Sing: Mater Dolorosa, Mother of Sorrows, you know our pain.

   *These prayers are adapted from *Your Sorrow Is My Sorrow,* Joyce Rupp (Crossroad
Publishing).

   ** Refer to the Appendix—Chants

Mary

133

Feast of the Mother of God

(Based on Luke 1:26-56; 2:1-21)

Mother of God, you risked saying yes to being pregnant with the seed of the Holy One,

> —may I also overcome my fears and take the risks that spiritual growth requires of me.

Mother of God, you offered the hospitality of your womb as a dwelling place for the Holy One,

> —may I continually open the womb of my heart to all who need a welcome there.

Mother of God, you awaited the long nine months of the child's gestation,

> —may I wait patiently when spiritual growth seems to come far too slowly.

Mother of God, you did not know how the birth of your child would affect your life,

> —may I trust in God's presence to protect and guide me when I face uncertainty.

Mother of God, you cared for and nurtured the divine life within you,

> —may I daily do the same through faithfulness to prayer and virtuous action.

Mother of God, you experienced the pain of contractions as you birthed the Holy One,

> —may I have the courage to bear the pains of my inner growth.

Mother of God, you found kinship with your pregnant cousin, Elizabeth,

> —may I recognize the Elizabeths who sustain and encourage me.

Mother of God, you felt the child within you stirring and kicking,

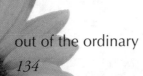

out of the ordinary

—may I deepen my awareness of God's stirrings in the midst of my life.

Mother of God, when the divine child pushed forth from your womb he uttered his first cry,

—may I believe in the goodness within me that is yet to resound.

Mother of God, the newly born child in your arms engendered awe, mystery, and wonder,

—may I, too, reverence and be awed by the way that the Divine One enters my life.

Ministry and Service

Discipleship

Suggestion for prayer: This service could be used by a group, with just one or two verses of each scripture being read followed by the prayer as a group response. Or it could be used by individuals, with one passage a day for meditation followed by the prayer for that day.

> They left everything
> and followed him.

—Luke 5:11

Luke 19:1-10

I am Zacchaeus. I, too, need to leave behind my concerns of what others will think of me. Jesus, when you approach my tree of life, when you ask to come to the home of my heart, may I be ready. Help me to respond to your call and to live the message of the gospel, even though I may experience criticism and rejection.

Luke 1:26-38

I am Mary of Nazareth. I must also leave some security behind. The challenge of the unknown is there for me. Jesus, you know the questions in my heart. When you send your messengers to me, I want to be open to receive them. May I say with deep trust in you, "Let what you have said be done in me."

John 21:15-23

I am Peter. I am asked to let go of my desire to be perfect and to live with my own unfinished condition. Jesus, you loved Peter as he was. You love me as I am. May I not only respond yes to your question, "Do you love me?" but also say yes when you take me "where I would rather not go."

Luke 5:27-28

I am Levi, the tax collector. I must leave behind my strong ambitions for success and power. Jesus, help me to be more concerned about the process of my life and ministry than about the results and

out of the ordinary

the success involved. Teach me what it means to leave everything and follow you.

John 4:1-42

I am the Samaritan woman. I am asked to leave behind my doubts about my own self-worth. Jesus, you called this woman to appreciate her own goodness. In my moments of self-doubt and hesitation, fill me with a disciple's heart. Help me to listen to you and to believe in your belief in me.

Luke 7:36-50

I am the woman who washed your feet, Jesus. You ask me to leave my old ways behind me. Fill me with true sorrow for the times when I have wandered far from you and your message. I, too, can experience the generosity of your forgiveness when I come to you with the tears of repentance.

John 11:1-44

I am Lazarus. I need the call to come out from my tomb. I must leave whatever is dead or binding for my spirit. Jesus, you call me daily to greater spiritual freedom. As your disciple, may I grow in my ability to have a discerning heart. May I, too, be unbound and "set free."

Prayer

Jesus, you call to my heart once more: "Leave anything that holds you back from deeper love. Come follow me, again and again." Grant me the courage to leave behind whatever keeps me from you and to trust you with my life. May my heart's connection with you be so strong and true that I will daily risk the road of following in your footsteps. Keep me open to the adventure of life where I meet you day by day. Remind me often of my inner goodness. Help me to believe that you look upon me with love. Thank you for the call to be your disciple. Amen.

To God Who Sings Through Us*

Leader

God who sings in our hearts, as the flute needs openness to receive the breath of melody, we pray to be open to the many ways that your symphony of love plays in our lives.

All — *Basses*

Thank you for the way that your enlivening Spirit touches us and moves through our beings. Remind us often that each one of us is a special instrument of yours. Together we create the wondrous music in your concert of love.

Leader

You stand at the door of our hearts, asking for an entrance. You desire to come in and share the intimacy of your presence with us (Rv 3:20).

All *Sopranos*

Behold, we open the door of our minds and hearts. We welcome your entrance and long for deeper union with you. Come and make music through our lives. Dance through our days and sing in our hearts.

Leader

We have days when we resist your movement and message. We seek you in stillness, but forget you in busyness. We yearn for fullness, but miss you in emptiness. We welcome you in joy, but reject you in sorrow. We rejoice in the harvest but struggle with the planting.

All — *Tenors*

Open our inner eyes so that we may know you in all the dimensions of our lives. Help us to trust you in the numerous ups and downs, to believe that your song can happen in all aspects of our existence.

out of the ordinary

140

Leader

God of courage and strength, we are waiting to receive your loving energy in the empty corners of our hearts. It is your power working through us that can do more than we can ever ask or imagine. It is your enlivening breath moving through us that enables us to overcome anxieties, fears, doubts, and misgivings (Eph 3:20).

All *Supos*

Breathe through us, Music Maker, and let your song weave a melody through all we are and do. May we acknowledge your power at work in us and open ourselves to this blessing.

Leader

You are a God who accepts the uniqueness and beauty of every individual. You love us as we are while you yearn for us to be more. You invite us to extend this kind of love to those who challenge our compassion and our patience. Your love within us will give us the strength to love them as we ought.

All

Nudge us and encourage us to accept those people who are alien to our love. May your song of kindness and patience be sung through us. Fill our attitude toward others with notes of understanding and nonjudgment.

*This prayer relates to the September theme "Instruments of God" in *May I Have This Dance?*, Joyce Rupp (Ave Maria Press).

Giving and Receiving

This prayer is based on the scriptural imperative to give of what we have received. Our gifts are recalled and named so we can see our abundance. We then respond with our willingness to share this abundance with others. Before this prayer, read these passages: Luke 6:37-38; Matthew 10:8. Take some time for dialogue to reflect upon individual gifts and talents among those who have gathered. For example: Name five gifts or talents for which you are particularly grateful; or, For which gift in your life are you most grateful?

Response to each: The gift I have received, I will give as a gift.

1. You have received mercy, kindness, and unconditional love from our God . . .

2. You have many physical, emotional, mental, and spiritual abilities that can be used to better the lives of others . . .

3. You have people in your life who have believed in you when you did not believe in yourself, people who stood by you in your difficult times . . .

4. You have a heart capable of great compassion, empathy, and tenderness . . .

5. You have inner strength, the grace of conversion, the gift of hope, and the desire for good . . .

6. You have food on your table, clothes in your closet, and a roof over your head . . .

7. You have access to medical care, good education, music and the arts, and numerous sources of communication . . .

8. You have religious freedom, the power of free speech, advocacy groups, and structures for promoting justice and protecting citizens . . .

9. You have a marvelous planet on which to live, with beautiful forests, rich soil for growing food, priceless minerals, precious creatures of all kinds . . .

10. You have the opportunity for spiritual renewal, growth, and maturity in your relationship with the divine, continual access to opportunities for faith development . . .

Together

Gracious Giver, so much has been bestowed upon me. I lack for little and yet yearn for so much. Continue to teach me to appreciate what has come to me as blessing and gift. Keep on urging and challenging me to share what I have. Help me to give generously and freely of my bounty. I offer you my thanks for all that has been granted to me. Amen.

Jesus, What Were the Pains of Your Ministry?

One day I reflected on how Jesus might have understood my ministerial struggles and concerns. I tried to "get inside his skin" and imagine what he must have felt like at times. I wondered if his experience was like mine. The following questions, as well as the questions about his joys which follow this section, came from that reflection.

—Did you ever feel that the people really didn't care about you, only about what you could do for them? Did you feel used when it became obvious that they wanted your gifts no matter what the cost to you?

—Were there times when you silently questioned whether you had the ability or talent to do what you felt compelled to do? Were you ever concerned about making mistakes or being a failure?

—When the crowds pressed against you, did you sometimes want to scream with the suffocating pressure of no solitude or space for yourself? Were you frustrated when you tried to be alone for a while and the people followed you to your quiet place?

—Was your heart ready to break with sorrow when you saw and heard the suffering and turmoil in people's lives?

—Were there times when you wondered what your life was about and if the pressure and rush of your work was worth it?

—Did you get discouraged when your work seemingly produced no results, or even worse, was refused by the very people you were giving all your energy to?

—Was there some fear and anxiety in you as you voiced your opinions about injustice and wrong use of power? Did you dread having to speak up for truth because of the possibility of rejection?

—Were you disillusioned or discouraged when your disciples missed your vision or failed to catch the deeper implications of your life and message?

—Did you ever get caught up in what others thought of you, especially when your own relatives and villagers couldn't understand what you were doing and why?

out of the ordinary

Jesus, mentor of my life, because you were fully human, you would have experienced many ups and downs in your work. Remind me on my difficult days, when I am involved with my work and bearing its pains, that you also had your share of these moments and moods. Help me to look deeper and to discover meaning and blessing in the journey of love and discipleship, even when there are trials and travails to bear.

Jesus, What Were the Joys of Your Ministry?

—Did your heart skip a beat when you realized how much power you had for healing? Did you want to leap for joy when you saw the immense happiness of those who had been restored to good health?

—Were you sometimes astounded at the strong, intense movement of generous love within you? Did this bountiful kindness pour easily into your relationships and amaze you with its beauty and goodness?

—What was it like to go alone to the mountains and be swept up in the Beloved's fondness for you? Was this one of those rare moments when everything in you settled into peacefulness? Did you leave with renewed passion for your work?

—Was the beauty of the earth a cause of hope for you? Did you have a sense of satisfaction as the sacredness and goodness of created things helped you find metaphors for your teachings?

—When you experienced men and women changing their lives for the better because of what you taught, were you filled with gratitude? Did these personal transformations, which your presence and message engendered, help you to accept the difficulties and struggles that went along with your ministry?

—Could you find enjoyment in the challenging conversations you had with your disciples and with strangers? Was it exciting and rewarding to discuss the brave opinions and ideas that you had?

—Did you find comfort and pleasure in your friendships? When you spent time with your close friends did you enjoy their presence and feel cherished? Did you have the joy of being happily welcomed by them any time you chose to be with them?

—Were you able to forget the tough parts of your work when you played with children, celebrated at weddings, walked through fields of ripened grain, and filled your eyes with the beauty of flowers?

—When you returned to your home in Nazareth did the smell of freshly baked bread and the strength of your mother's welcoming embrace help you to feel cherished? Did your visits with her nourish both your body and spirit?

out of the ordinary

Jesus, help me to enter into the joyful dimensions of my work. Let me not be so involved and serious about my work that I miss the many pleasures and joys that are inherent in it. Lighten me up when I am feeling my work's heaviness. May I remember that I need balance in my life, that laughter and leisure are essential for my total health. Take me to sources of zest and enthusiasm without guilt or hesitation. May my work become one of the playgrounds of my life.

A Disciple's Prayer

How easy to believe that I am an instrument of your love when my life is going well, O God. How difficult to believe this when my life seems to be going nowhere, or is filled with many concerns and activities that wear me out. Yet, you greatly desire to proclaim your goodness through every part of my life, no matter what the situation is.

I do not need to have good feelings in order to be an instrument of your love. I do not need to always feel satisfied with what I am attempting to be and to do in order to be a disciple of yours. It is the intention of my heart that makes the difference. Deep within I long for you and I give myself to your cause. I place my heart in yours and enter as fully as I can into your loving embrace.

I am your messenger, ready to tell of your enormous kindness and mercy. I will trust in you. I believe that those with whom I live and work will see your love shining through all I am and all I do. It is your radiance within me that will transform the bits and pieces of my life into a tapestry of ardent devotion. Thank you for being present in my life and for calling to me with your gracious voice of unconditional love. Amen.

Take Nothing for the Journey

Then Jesus called the twelve together . . . and he sent them
out to proclaim the kingdom of God and to heal. He said
to them, "Take nothing for your journey. . . ."

—Luke 9:1-6

Heal and proclaim . . .
Were the twelve afraid?
Did they wonder if they could do those things?
Compared to the quality of your ministry,
did they feel inadequate and unworthy?
What persuaded them to go? Your words?
Your friendship? Their enthusiasm?
Your deep belief that they could do it?

And you said:
"Take nothing for the journey."
What did you mean?
Trust or more than trust?
Did you perhaps imply that we can't wait
until we have all the possible things we need?
That we can't postpone "doing"
until we are positive of our talents?
That we can't hold off our commitment
until we are absolutely sure
we won't make a mistake?

I think of all the excuses and reasons
we can give for not serving and giving:
no time, no talent, no knowledge,
no energy, no assured results.
You say, "Take nothing.
Don't worry about your inadequacies.
I will provide for you.
Go! Just go! Go with my power.

Risk the road, risk the work.
Go! I will be with you.
What else do you need?"

—Joyce Rupp

Called Forth*

God called out to him out of the bush, "Moses, Moses! . . .
Remove the sandals from your feet,
for the place on which you are standing is holy ground.

—Exodus 3:4-5

There's a burning bush in me, Pilgrim God. It is the flame of your presence in my quite ordinary moments. Your indwelling makes all of my life an opportunity for sacred encounter. Thank you for the burning-bush moments I have known. Each one draws me more closely to your heart and increases my awareness of the beauty of your eternal faithfulness.

Then Mary said, "Here I am, the servant of [God];
let it be with me according to your word (Lk 1:38).

Mystery penetrates every aspect of my life with you, Divine Secret. I cannot know or understand where the call to be yours will take me. I do not need to know, even though I *want* to know. All that is required is that I trust you with my life. Wrap your love around me so completely that I will readily give you my "yes."

Then one of the seraphs flew to me, holding a live
coal. . . .
The seraph touched my mouth with it . . . (Is 6:6-7).

I, too, am being refined as you call me to live a deeper life. It is the purification of my motives and my expectations in living and working with others. It is the cleansing of my mind and heart of all that keeps me from clearly and freely being one with you. Divine Ember, burn away all in me that keeps me from saying, "Here I am. I am yours."

O [God], you have enticed me, and I was enticed;
you have overpowered me,
and you have prevailed (Jer 20:7).

I sometimes protest the call to be your presence in the world. Like Jeremiah, my voice cries out in protest and my heart refuses to respond. I am unable to go in your name because I ignore your powerful love flowing through me. I think that I have to go alone, and I grow unsure, full of questions and doubts. Enduring One, sweep my heart free of my arrogant independence and keep urging me toward acceptance of your grace.

> Mary Magdalene went and announced to the disciples,
> "I have seen the Lord"; and she told them that
> he had said these things to her (Jn 20:18).

There is an announcement time for me, Intimate Friend. It comes each time I meet you in the garden of my life. Every encounter with you is an opportunity to recognize you and to accept your divine manifestation, however ecstatic or simple it may be. You encourage me to find you amid the people and events of each day. Show yourself to me and, then, send me forth!

> She said to the people,
> "Come and see . . ." (Jn 4:28-29).

Source of Life and Love, you call me to bear witness to you. Everywhere I go, with all whom I meet, the bond of your love unites us. In those I resist, in those who resist me, in those I welcome, in those who welcome me—in all I meet, there you are! Grant me eyes of the heart so that I may see deeply, that I may discover and reverence each one who is a part of my life. Grant me a courageous spirit so that I will live in such a way that all will know that you are the center of my life.

* An appropriate chant to use with this is "Here I Am," c.f. Appendix—Chants.

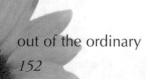

out of the ordinary

The Continuous Call to Conversion

I am convinced that all human beings
have an inborn desire for God . . .
this desire is our deepest longing
and our most precious treasure.

—Gerald May

Mentor of my life, you invite me to follow you. You give me the courage to do so. It is risky to go in your way. Help me to trust in you, especially on those days when I feel a lack of security or when I face the challenge of standing up for your truth.

Merciful One, there have been times when I have made choices and decisions that were not in keeping with the message and values of your son, Jesus. Forgive me for the distance that I place between you and myself. Keep calling me home to you when I get lost on the road to your love.

Faithful God, your forgiveness and love are powerful reminders of who you are. As I experience your goodness through the sacraments, people, nature, and events of my days, draw me ever nearer to your heart. Deepen in me a desire to share this love with others.

It is sometimes difficult to believe that you love me as much as you do, Beloved One. I am humbled to know that you accept me with my weaknesses and my incompleteness. It is this tremendous love of yours which invites a welcoming response from me. Help me to say with my whole heart, "I receive your great love with gratitude."

God of light, open me to see the many ways that you are present in my life. Light my way. Guide me. Gift me with an inner eye of faith so that all of life takes on the quality of your loving presence.

May the power of your Spirit fill me with a desire to follow you, Divine Companion. Help me to renew my commitment to you day by day. As I continue on the journey of life, fill me with gratitude for the power of your love stirring within me. Unite me with all who need your loving touch through my care and compassion.

Put Out Into the Deep Waters

(A Guided Visualization of Luke 5:1-11)

Read the story in its entirety. Then, go back and re-read verses 1-3.

Imagine that you are there in the scene. Visualize what it is like:
Jesus by the lake . . . the smell of fish and salt of the sea . . .
The blue sky and warm sun on your body . . . a slight breeze moves
  across your face . . .
The crowd around you . . . eager to see, hear, and touch Jesus.
They are pressing and pushing to get closer . . .
The smell of sweat and dust . . . a sense of anticipation and excitement.
You look at Jesus there before you . . . you hear him—his voice is
  firm and strong
yet there's also a quality of care and concern. . . .
His voice tells you he is convinced of his message and he yearns for
  you to hear it.

Jesus pauses, distracted by the two boats that have pulled up by the
  bank of the lake. . . .
There are fishermen washing their nets in the lake by the boat. . . .
Hear the swish of the nets in the water . . . see the nets lifted up and
  down . . .
Smell the fish and the sea. . . .
Jesus walks over to the boats . . . you watch him. . . .
Hear him ask Simon if he can get into the boat . . . he asks Simon
  to put out a bit from shore.

Jesus sits in the boat . . . contented and ready to teach again.
He starts to speak . . . you listen closely. . . . This time, the words
  sink into your heart.
What does Jesus say to you that you need so much to hear?
Pause to write down what you hear Jesus saying to you.

Continue with the visualization by re-reading verses 4-11.

Imagine that you are Simon, Peter. . . . Jesus tells you to go out into
  the deep water. . . .
Then he tells you to put your net into the deep water. . . .
You remember how you worked all night and caught nothing. . . .

out of the ordinary

You can feel your sore muscles and your tired eyes,
but you are drawn by Jesus and his insistence. . . .
So you toss the nets in . . . hear the net splash, see it sink. . . .
What are you thinking as you toss the net in and wait?

You begin to pull the net back in. . . .
It is so heavy you can hardly pull on it and your heart beats faster
and faster. . . .
You call those in the other boat to come and help you. . . .
Together you haul the net close to the boats . . .
and then you toss fish after fish after fish into the boat. . . .
You are surrounded by fish everywhere in the boat. . . .
Everyone is full of surprise . . . you can hardly believe what is
happening. . . .
Then you look up at Jesus . . . you see joy, love, and delight on his
face. . . .
He seems to look straight into your heart. . . .
Suddenly you feel humbled and awed by the presence of such a
powerful love. . . .
Jesus reaches out and touches you on the arm, takes your hand. . . .
He speaks to you: "Will you leave your old things behind and follow
me?
Will you join with me in my life and work? Will you come with me?"

You go to the shore with Jesus. . . . You ask to sit down and talk
with him. . . .
Spend some time in dialogue with Jesus about the invitation he has
given to you. . . .
You might reflect upon the following:
What "old things" do you need to leave behind?
What might the "deep waters" be for you?
What would you hope to find in the "deep waters"?

Write your response to Jesus' question: Will you come with me?

Close with thanking Jesus for the time you have spent with him and
see yourself walking along the shore of the lake with him.

Ministry and Service

Catechist's Prayer

Great Teacher, how can it be September already?
It seems just yesterday that my last class ended.
You know how busy and filled with rush my days are,
how often I run without remembering your nearness.
Keep me more faithful to those quiet times with you
and more alert to your presence amid my activities.

As I anticipate teaching another class this year,
there's a part of me that's fearful and anxious,
doubting that I've faith enough to be the one to share it.
Take that doubt, Companion of Love, and change it.
Help me to see that I do believe, that my faith is deep,
if I but take the time to touch it with prayerful reflection.

There's a part of me that's uncertain and concerned,
wondering if my hard work will be worth the effort.
How will I know if my ministry has made a difference?
Take this concern from my troubled heart, Peaceful One.
Help me to recognize that you never leave me.
It is your compassionate presence dwelling within me
that will call to young hearts and lead them home to you.
You will do so in a way that may never be known to me.

Divine Life-Giver, when I become tired and drained,
be the energy and aliveness that I need.
Grant me the grace of enthusiasm,
so the love I have for you will shine through me.

Most of all, Sacred Echo of Happiness, be joy in me.
Do not let me give in to the demon of discouragement.
Rather, remind me often that I am your instrument,
blessed with the gift of wanting to share my faith
and privileged to be in communion with your loved ones.

I need only to open my shaky heart to you.
I need only to surrender my spirit in trust.
I need only to cry out to you in prayer.
You will be there, you will hear my needs.
You will walk with me each step of the way,
touching all those who are entrusted to my care.

—Joyce Rupp

The New Year

The New Year

Faithful Companion,
in this new year I pray:

to live deeply, with purpose,
to live freely, with detachment,
to live wisely, with humility,
to live justly, with compassion,
to live lovingly, with fidelity,
to live mindfully, with awareness,
to live gratefully, with generosity,
to live fully, with enthusiasm.

Help me to hold this vision
and to daily renew it in my heart,
becoming ever more one with you,
my truest Self.

—Joyce Rupp

I Arise in the New Year

One year I observed what I felt was arising in my spirit as I greeted the Holy One on that first day of the new year. I suggest that you also reflect on what is arising within you. Don't think too hard about it. Just let it be a spontaneous naming of your awareness.

I arise with **amazement** at the presence of the Holy One.

I arise with **gratitude** for life.

I arise with **hope** that all shall be well.

I arise with **courage** to meet what will be difficult.

I arise with **conviction** to do what is life-giving.

I arise with **eyes ever alert** for beauty.

I arise with **openness** to greater truth.

I arise with **desire** for continued transformation.

I arise with **compassion** for the hurting ones in the cosmos.

I arise with **grief** still settled in my spirit.

I arise with **eagerness** to write with depth and quality.

I arise with **a sense of kinship** with all whom I love.

I arise with **respect** as others mentor and deepen my vision.

I arise with **determination** to make good choices in using my time.

I arise with **willingness to help** those who will need my care.

I arise with **hesitation** as I think about pain that may come.

I arise with **longing** for ever greater inner freedom.

I arise with **happiness**, knowing I am invited to live life fully.

I arise with **love** for the Holy One, my Intimate Companion.

Compassionate Companion and Faithful Friend, thank you for the opportunity to walk into another year of life. Help me to be faithful, to be generous, to be yours.

The New Year

Reflection on a New Year

The beginning of a new year always merits some reflection. It is not so much a time of making new resolutions, but rather, space in which to ponder life and review personal growth. A new year is a good opportunity to look at what guides my thoughts and decisions each day, to look at the person I already am and who I want to become.

As I review the year, I look for what allows my life to receive greater meaning and what resists it. I ponder how and when hope has sung in my days. I wander through the months recalling who and what gave me strength and where enthusiasm ripened or died on the vine. I look for graced moments that I have totally forgotten, those spaces in my days when I am swept off my controlled feet by the grace of a tender God who says, "Don't forget you are in my heart."

When I review my journal from the past year I often see that there's a part of it filled with familiar melodies, some delightful and others quite jarring. My insights and awareness touch again and again on some basic patterns and behaviors. When I see them, I sometimes say with a groan, "I've been here before!" However, I have noticed that almost every time I come around the circle I know it better. I miss more of the off-key notes and disharmony as I get better acquainted with their positions and characteristics, so I feel a sense of hope in spite of the old recurring patterns.

Underneath the circle of my year, I can always spot my life principles—the foundational themes and values that spur me on to live my dreams and rekindle a positive attitude. One year I rediscovered a life principle when I received a Christmas gift that was truly given from the heart. I was at the home of a five-year-old girl whose shining eyes and bright smile could shake the world awake with joy. As I entered her house she went running to her room and came out beaming, carrying her gift to me on a used Christmas card: nine recently found pennies and two uneaten peanuts! A widow's mite, to be sure. Nothing could have made me happier.

On New Year's Day that year, I rearranged my inner world a bit to make room again for offering little kindnesses to others. I saw my all too familiar pattern of being too busy for even a smile when I am

out of the ordinary

rushed and pressed for time. I renewed my life principle of being a woman of loving kindness. I asked for the grace to give my own nine pennies and two peanuts to each person I met in the coming year.

Standing at the Gates of the New Year

Sacred Mystery,
waiting on the threshold
of this new year,
you open the gates
and beckon to me:

"Come! Come!
Be not wary of what awaits you
as you enter the unknown terrain,
be not doubtful of your ability
to grow from its joys and sorrows.

For I am with you.
I will be your Guide.
I will be your Protector.
You will never be alone."

Guardian of this new year,
I set aside my fears, worries, concerns,
I open my life to mystery, to beauty,
to hospitality, to questions,
to the endless opportunity
of discovering you in my relationships,
and to all the silent wisps of wonder
that will draw me to your heart.

I welcome your unfailing Presence
and walk with hope into this new year.

—Joyce Rupp

A New Year's Meditation

As you look back on the year just completed:

1. What name would you give to your journey of the past year? How would you describe it to one of your friends? What image or metaphor would you use to talk about it?

2. What were some of your "epiphanies" of the past year (your discoveries of the Holy One in your midst)? How did you grow because of them?

3. Who were your wise persons? What did they reveal to you? How did this influence your life?

4. Did any of your hopes and dreams become a reality?

5. What was most satisfying about the year? What was least satisfying?

6. How did your experience of the past year affect the world in which you live?

As you look to the year before you:

1. What name would you like your new year's journey to have? What gifts do you bring with you into the year before you?

2. Do you find any resistance within you? Of what are you most afraid as you enter a new year?

3. What is your greatest need for the coming year?

4. Who do you bring with you for your support and strength as you begin to journey through the year?

5. How is your relationship with the Holy One as you pause on the threshold of the new year's vast landscape? What is at the heart of your new year's prayer?

6. What do you hope to contribute to society in this coming year?

The New Year

The Old Year Runs Away From Me

the old year runs away from me.
I hang onto her sleeve
but she shakes me loose.
where does the old year go
when the new year comes?

she slips away into memories,
falls into the crevices of wishes
and ought-to-have-dones.
she waits no longer upon promises,
turns her back on might-have-been.

the elves of the old year step in,
pack up the struggles, store the joys,
tuck them away in the bulging box
spreading out on the psyche's floor.

it's up to the new year now.
I bring a lot to her domain:
expectations, dreams, hopes,
and I place them all before
her strong, abundant door.

I walk into her untamed territory,
with a meek apprehension
and a vast sense of mystery,
assured by the welcome I receive,

anxious about what is waiting
behind the drawn window shade,
curious about what I will discover
in the hidden folds of her new days.

—Joyce Rupp

Leaving the Old, Welcoming the New

Go to your place of prayer where you can be alone in stillness.

Begin by quieting your body and mind. It is helpful to do this by taking in a deep breath and letting it out slowly. (Do this three or four times.)

Recall the presence of the Holy One dwelling in love within you.

Turn your heart to remembrance of how this Holy One shelters you.

Place your hands on your lap, palms up and open.

Mentally place in your hands these people and events of the past year:

> . . . your loved ones,
>
> . . . your colleagues and coworkers,
>
> . . . those for whom you were responsible to offer care and concern,
>
> . . . those with whom you have had differences and struggles,
>
> . . . all people, events, and situations that held significance for you,
>
> . . . anyone or anything else that comes to your mind or heart.

Now mentally place in your open hands all of your gifts of the past year:

> . . . your happinesses,
>
> . . . your successes,
>
> . . . your insights and awareness,
>
> . . . your messengers from the Holy One,
>
> . . . your difficult things that helped you to grow,
>
> . . . whatever else seems like a gift to you.

Offer your prayer of gratitude for the year just completed, with all its blessings and opportunities for growth. *You might want to pause here and write a prayer.*

Next, place in your open hands:

>   . . . your whole life, all your concerns, cares, hopes, dreams, joys,

>   . . . any specific persons with whom you feel especially bonded, or hope to be, in the new year,

>   . . . the beauty of earth,

>   . . . anything or anyone else whom you are especially mindful of bringing into the new year with you.

Entrust yourself to the Holy One. Pray your prayer of hope as you begin the new year. *You may want to pause and write this prayer of hope.*

To close this time of prayer, stand, raise your hands (palms up). Hold them high in the air. Once again, place all of your life in those hands and give all to the Holy One. Then bow to the Holy One who dwells within you. Go with peace and hope into the new year.

Other

Magnificat to the God of Dawn

My being proclaims the wonders of light
as it slowly penetrates the ebbing darkness

And my spirit bows to the beauty of the One
who gives life to all that has existence

Oh, vibrant green stems of life sing out
your praise to the Heart who draws you forth

Bird songs rejoicing in the breath of dawn,
warble your joy in view of the morning star

Dew drops radiant upon the wetness of grass
give glory to the Wise Creator who sustains you

Flower gardens, rushing streams, silent deserts,
sing, sing, for the Dancer who rejoices in your midst

Peoples of the planet, creatures of the universe,
play before the Enlivener who delights in you

And my soul, my soul, rise up and greet this day
with gratitude, in a stance of humble remembering

For all I am, and all I am called to be, is held
in the hands of a Creator who daily loves me into life

—Joyce Rupp

Six Gestures of the Morning Praise

Each morning when I arise I begin the day with these six gestures. I join spirit and body in praising the Holy One and offering my thanks for life. As I do the gestures I say a one line prayer and then remain in that posture for a brief time.

1. Offering the Creator praise and gratitude:
    Stretch your arms high and wide above your head.
    I thank you, Holy One, for the gift of another day of life.

2. Intentionally being aware of my spiritual bond with all of creation:
    Hold arms out from your sides, a little below shoulder height. Move (pivot) to the left and to the right with your arms stretching outward toward the cosmos.
    I reach out in compassion to my sisters and brothers throughout the universe.

3. Offering my life to the Holy One:
    Stretch your arms out straight in front of you, slightly apart, palms up.
    I give to you all I am and all I have.

4. Opening to accept what the Holy One offers me this day:
    Pull your hands close together and cup them as a container.
    I open my entire being to receive the gift that you have waiting for me in this new day.

5. Remembering to be kind to our planet Earth:
    Bend over, reach down, and touch the floor, or better yet, the ground, if you are outside.
    I touch this planet, Earth, with awe, reverence, and gratitude, promising to care well for her today.

6. Awareness of the indwelling presence of the Holy One:
    Stand up, cross hands over your heart, and bow to the waist.
    May I be united with you throughout this day, aware of your love strengthening me and shining through me.

Blessing for a Newly Birthed Child

The child's name is spoken before each blessing. The mother holds the child while the father, or other designated person, proclaims the blessings.

(Name), may the miracle of your birth always be a source of joy for you.

_____, may you be blessed by wise, caring people who will guide you and protect you.

_____, may you always keep your openness to wonder and new discoveries.

_____, may you have a healthy body, a keen mind, an adventurous spirit, and a deeply caring heart.

_____, may you be treasured by your family and by all who take care of you.

_____, may you be filled with wonderful dreams and dance through life as a child of the universe.

_____, may you have many friends and be a good friend in return.

_____, may you believe in your goodness and value your self-worth.

_____, may you be aware of the tremendous love that the Creator has for you.

The father now holds the child up high toward the sky while the mother, or other designated person, prays the following:

Holy One, we entrust our child into your gracious care.

Compassionate One, shelter our beloved daughter (son) throughout her (his) life.

Sibling response*

Beloved of the Soul, fill our child with a deep sense of your radiant presence.

Sibling response*

Creator of the universe, gift our child with the twinkling laughter of the stars.

out of the ordinary

*Sibling response**

Eternal Parent, our child is your child. Guide and direct us as we nurture our daughter (son) with the qualities she (he) needs to live life to the fullest.

*Sibling response**

Thank you for the wonderful gift of this child. We know we are richly blessed. Amen.

* Sibling response: If there are siblings, each one could hold a balloon and, at the designated places, wave their balloons and give a cheer: "Yea, God! Thank you for _____ (name of child being blessed)."

A Parish Centennial Prayer

Gatherer of All Good Memories,
the spirits of many ancestors join us
here in this sacred place of _____ *(name of parish)*.
We have come to celebrate a history,
to gather the memories of many decades.

You have been a Companion for each one:
every grandfather and grandmother,
every student and teacher,
every single person, every priest, and nun,
every father and mother, brother and sister.

You have been the Breath of Life
for everyone who has birthed a child,
wedded a lover, or buried a dear one.

You have sown the deep seeds of faith
in the waters of countless baptisms,
kept alive a parish for a hundred years
through the fidelity of those who prayed here,
and the generosity of those who served here.

While our world is weary and worn with pain,
may we take hope and find courage
in what we celebrate:
the strong faith of our ancestors,
the friendship of neighbors and relatives,
the generous leadership of pastors,
the goodness of each one willing to reach out
and be there in a time of need.

We thank you, Gracious God, for our faith,
and for this place of worship and community,
which has nourished many souls,
and provided a source of nurturing faith
for all who came seeking spiritual life.

May we leave here filled with hope,
knowing that the people of _____ *(name of parish)*
believed in your constant Presence,
accepted your Grace, shared your Love,
and celebrated your Life with one another. Amen.

—Joyce Rupp

The Twelve Steps Prayer

Each of the twelve steps is listed before the prayer associated with that step.

1. *We admitted we were powerless over our addiction—that our lives had become unmanageable.*

You are my strength, O Divine Being. You are my Inward Source of Love, gracing my life. You give me the spiritual energy I need to overcome all that keeps me from being more fully yours.

2. *Came to believe that a Power greater than ourselves could restore us to sanity.*

On those days when I think that I can go it alone and when I want to rely on only myself, draw me to you, Spirit of Life. Remind me of this basic, essential truth: you are the way to my inner serenity and peace.

3. *Made a decision to turn our will and our lives over to the care of God as we understood God.*

I desire to surrender my whole and entire self to you, my Higher Power. Take the fear and shame in me and help me to entrust myself to you.

4. *Made a searching and fearless moral inventory of ourselves.*

As I continue to look into my life, grant me honesty so that I can see myself as I truly am: to claim my goodness and my greatness, to recognize my compulsions and my weaknesses.

5. *Admitted to God, to ourselves, and to another human being the exact nature of our wrongs.*

Surround me with your love, O Beloved, as I tell you, and others, the truth of my addictive behavior and the reality of my failures. May your gift of courage lead me to the freeing of my heart and a greater openness to receive your love.

6. *Were entirely ready to have God remove all these defects of character.*

Keep me open and ready to let go of whatever it is that needs to be given up, given over, and given away. Give me strength to not cling to, hoard, or hide what keeps me wounded and fettered to my addictions.

7. Humbly asked God to remove our shortcomings.

I stand ready to be transformed in and through your love. I know that you yearn for me to be more whole. Deepen my awareness of your healing forgiveness and grant me the gift of forgiving myself.

8. Made a list of all persons we had harmed, and became willing to make amends to them all.

I remember all those whom I may have harmed by my failures, faults, and unhealthy behavior. I bring them to you, Liberating One, asking that you extend your blessing of love upon them.

9. Made direct amends to such people whenever possible, except when to do so would injure them or others.

Grant me the courage to reach out to those in my life who have been affected by my lack of spiritual freedom, Compassionate One. Lead me to ways that will promote goodness and well-being for them.

10. Continued to take personal inventory and when we were wrong promptly admitted it.

Divine Guide, help me to be aware of my compulsions and unhealthy actions when they push forth and wound others or myself. Remind me often that I am always unfinished, that I will constantly need you by my side in order to make good choices for my life.

11. Sought through prayer and meditation to improve our conscious contact with God as we understood God, praying only for knowledge of God's will for us and the power to carry that out.

In my busy and stressful times, draw me to you, Abiding Peace. May I find time each day for union with you in meditation and prayer. Continue to convince me of how essential this bond with you is.

12. Having had a spiritual awakening as the result of these steps, we tried to carry this message to those addicted, and to practice these principles in all our affairs.

Indwelling Strength, as I live these truths through what I say and do, may I be mindful that your grace is sufficient for me, that your power working through me can do more than I can ever ask or imagine (2 Cor 12:9; Eph 3:20).

—Joyce Rupp

Other

Blessing of the Body

This blessing is designed for use with groups, inviting those present to each find a partner to bless. However, it could also be used by just two persons, with one blessing the other. When used with groups, partners should face each other and then ask about the other person's comfortableness with being touched. If he or she prefers a non-touch blessing, the other person can simply hold his or her hand near the part of the body being blessed, rather than touching it. As the leader prays each blessing out loud the couples silently bless one another at the same time. For the last part, each phrase or sentence is repeated after the leader.

Forehead: May you have keen insights and think clearly. May your thoughts be kind and wise. May you resolve anything in your mind that keeps you from being your true self.

Ears: May you listen to the inner Voice of the Beloved and act on the word of God. May you hear the melodies of your own goodness and treasure who you are.

Eyes: May you have inner vision to see more clearly the path that is yours. May you look upon others with love as you search for your way home.

Mouth: May you speak with love, proclaim the truth, and make your needs known. May you laugh at the absurdities of life and taste life with joy and enthusiasm.

Nose: As you take in air and let out air, may you be reminded of the cycle of life with its dying and rising, it's emptying and filling. May you breathe in the aroma of goodness and breathe out what needs to be let go.

Hands: May you use your hands to touch all of life with reverence and gratitude. May these hands reach out with care to others. May these hands be willing to receive from others.

Skin: May you be not too thick-skinned or too thin-skinned as you journey. May you reverence and protect the dignity of others no matter what color of skin they have.

Heart: May you develop awareness of what stirs deep within you. May you have a vibrant, compassionate heart, one that is filled with generosity and kindness.

Feet: As you travel through the many ups and downs of life, may all the places your feet take you lead you to greater transformation and inner freedom. May you develop an ever firmer foundation for your spiritual path.

Leader

I invite each of you now to repeat what I will say. Whisper these words into the ear of your partner. To do so, you will need to be very close to each other.

May the shelter of God embrace you in your difficult moments.

May the Dance of God play in your joyful moments.

May the Peace of God be with you wherever you are on your journey of life.

Amen!

Family Reunion

Leader

Gracious and loving God, we gather here today to celebrate our common bond as descendants of the *(family name)* family. As we do so, we remember all those men and women who have gone before us, leaving us the treasured memories of their lives. We recall how blessed we are to be a part of this journey of life. May our time together be a source of joy and hope for each one here.

All

We come with our own story of life. We bring with us our joys and sorrows, our trials and our successes. We come here knowing that the bond of history and of blood unites us. If there are differences that divide us, we pray that we will set them aside this day and welcome each one who is with us. We join in celebrating all the blessings which our ancestors have left us.

Leader

I invite you now to hold high any newborn infants or small children who were not with us the last time we met for a reunion. Let the other young children come to the front of our gathering *(allow time for the gathering and holding up of the children).*

Please repeat after me as you extend your hands toward these children:

> God of life . . . we behold those who will carry on our family ancestry. . . . Gift them with a great love of life . . . and a deep faith. . . . May they know the blessings of our ancestors. . . . May they appreciate what has been handed down to them. . . . Thank you for these young treasures. . . . Amen!

Blessed be the ties that bind us and blessed be our God for the many gifts given to us. We join now in thanking God for the food we are about to share.

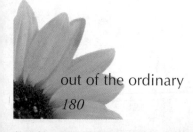

out of the ordinary

All

Bless us, and these gifts of nourishment and of celebration, which we are about to receive. We thank you. Amen.

All join in singing to the tune of "Morning Has Broken."

1. Now we are gathered/at this reunion,
   Let us remember/how we are one.
   We have been given/the people around us,
   Let us give thanks, then,/for this great gift.

2. Soon we will share in/the food at this table,
   Soon we'll be telling/stories of old.
   As we remember/all that's been given,
   We can be thankful/for all these gifts.

The Seven Steps of Morning *

*If praying alone, one can do this walking around any room, taking very small, contemplative steps. If praying with a group, all form a circle and face clockwise, moving in that direction. One small step is taken for each of the seven words. After the word is announced, one small step is taken. Then the word "gratitude," "love," or some other is repeated quietly several times. Stay for one or two minutes with the word. Then the next step is taken, the word is announced, repeated, etc. ***

My (our) first step is that of **gratitude** . . . for the gift of another fresh day of life.

My (our) second step is that of **love** . . . for the Holy One and for all of my dear ones.

My third step is that of **hope** . . . for the possibility of growth in each moment.

My fourth step is that of **compassion** . . . for all of creation and our deep connection.

My fifth step is that of **generosity** . . . for all that shall be asked of me this day.

My sixth step is that of **laughter** . . . for the joys that will refresh my heart.

My seventh step is that of **patience** . . . for the difficult challenges that may arise.

Giver of Life, awaken my (our) entire being so that I (we) can enter this day with the eagerness of one who sees beauty and truth strewn through every part of life. Deepen my (our) bond with you and strengthen my (our) peace. Amen.

Some other qualities that might be inserted in place of these seven: trust, nonjudgment, recovery, strength, kindness, faith, fidelity, hope, healing, etc.

* A chant that can be used to open this morning prayer is "I Am Alive" (see Appendix—Chants). It can be sung facing the four directions of east, south, west, and north. The chant is sung once for each direction.

out of the ordinary

* * I first began using "seven steps" as a morning prayer. I chose seven because it is a symbol of wholeness. I have since created many other "seven steps" for other types of occasions. I encourage you to be creative and compose your own seven steps for birthdays, transitions, anniversaries, etc. Also, be in touch with your emotional, spiritual space. You may have a day (or month!) in which all seven words are the same, e.g., "patience" would be announced and repeated for each of the seven steps.

Other

Praying With the Five Senses

Smell, Taste, See, Hear, Touch

To understand the world knowledge is not enough;
you must see it, touch it, live in its presence and drink
the vital heat of existence in the very heart of reality.

—Pierre Teilhard de Chardin

Smell/Breathe

Then [God] formed [humankind] from the dust of the ground, and breathed into [humankind's] nostrils the breath of life (Gn 2:7).

Let my prayer be counted as incense before you (Ps 141:2).

Do: Go for a walk. Give yourself the gift of breathing.
Notice your breath; celebrate the fact that you are alive.
Be aware of breathing in life and breathing out what is not life-giving.

Reflect: What is the incense of your life that is being offered to God?

Prayer (see below)

Taste/Savor

Taste and see that [God] is good (Ps 34:8).

I would feed you with the finest of the wheat, and with honey from the rock I would satisfy you (Ps 81:16).

Do: As you eat your meals today, savor every bite.
Take time to enjoy all the different flavors. Chew slowly.
Be grateful for the gift of nourishment on all levels of your life.

Reflect: What does the goodness of God taste like to you?

Prayer (see below)

See/Observe

So I have looked upon you in the sanctuary (Ps 63:2).

Jesus, looking at him, loved him (Mk 10:21).

out of the ordinary

Do: Find something in nature. Look long at it.
Befriend it. See all of its details (size, shape, color, texture, etc.).
Then, take a piece of paper and sketch it.

Reflect: What do you see of God's presence in your life?
How do you look upon others with love?

Prayer (see below)

Hear/Listen

Listen carefully to me. . . . Incline your ear, and come to me; listen, so that you may live (Is 55:2-3).

Your servant is listening (1 Sm 3:10).

Do: Sit very, very quietly. Be still. Listen to all the sounds around you.
Listen to all the sounds that are within you.
After your time of listening, make a list of what you have heard.

Reflect: What do you hear in the silence of your heart?

Prayer (see below)

Touch/Feel

I was to them like those who lift infants to their cheeks (Hos 11:4).

But Jesus said, "Someone touched me; for I noticed that power had gone out from me" (Lk 8:46).

Do: Spend time with your hands. Touch the texture of skin;
notice the bumps, ridges, contours; feel the shape and size of
your hands. Close your eyes and touch your hands again.
Imagine God holding your hands.

Reflect: What does God's hand in your hand feel like?

Prayer (see below)

Prayer after each reflection with one of the five senses:

Sensual Life-giver, you have created me wonderfully. Awaken me through my five senses. Surprise me, entice me! Draw me into gratitude and awe! Thank you for these gifts of my body and for all they teach me about you.

Other

Blessing of a House

For this blessing you will need one large lit candle that can be carried from room to room without spilling the wax; you will also need to select a "candle carrier" and a leader. All present go from room to room and gather around the lit candle in each designated section of the house as it is blessed. The "Residents" response is prayed by those who are going to reside in the house. The "All" response is prayed by all who are gathered.

Invocation

Gather outside the front of the house (or outside the front door of the apartment.) Light the candle that will be carried.

Leader

Unless [God] builds the house, those who build it labor in vain (Ps 127:1).

Residents *(the residents of the house or apartment)*

O God, we (I) desire to have you as the firm foundation of our lives. May what we experience in this residence be a source of harmony and happiness for us. As we find shelter here, may we also find shelter in your abiding love.

All

Make this house a home! (All those gathered voice this response after each time the residents pray.)

Blessing of the Front Door *(Stand outside the front door)*

Leader

Jesus said: "Abide in me as I abide in you" (Jn 15:4).

Residents

Companion on our journey, you have made a home in our hearts. As we gather to bless this space, may our union with you help this house to become a home. May all who enter here be as welcome in our hearts as we are in yours.

All except the candle bearer extend hands toward the front door; the leader opens the door.

Welcoming God, we open this front door as a sign of the openness of our hearts. May each one who enters here be received with the warmth of your kindness. As each one leaves, may they have experienced the blessedness of your gracious presence in us.

Blessing of the Kitchen

Leader

I will bless [God] at all times, [God's] praise shall continually be in my mouth.

O taste and see that [God] is good (Ps 34:1, 8).

Residents

Bread of Life, may the food that is prepared in this room be a source of strength for both our physical and our spiritual life. May all that takes place here remind us of the many times and ways that you nourish us consistently and generously.

Blessing of the Dining Room

Leader

How precious is your steadfast love, O God!
All people may take refuge in the shadow of your wings.
They feast on the abundance of your house,
and you give them drink from the river of your delights (Ps 36:7-8).

Residents

Nourishing God, we anticipate with love all who will gather at this table. May the conversations we share and the food we eat bring us happiness and contentment. May any discord and quarrels at this table be solved with kindness and openness.

Blessing of the Bathroom

Leader

Create in me, a clean heart, O God,
and put a new and right spirit within me (Ps 51:10).

Residents

May each bodily activity that takes place here remind us to treat our bodies kindly. As we shave, shampoo, shower or bathe, cleanse our spirits as well as our bodies. As we eliminate waste from our bodies may we also choose to let go of any mental and emotional refuse that is no longer helpful for our spiritual life.

Blessing of the Laundry

Leader

Prosper the work of our hands, O God, prosper the work of our hands (Ps 90:17).

Residents

May all who use this room, or benefit from the washing and drying that is done here, find joy in their life and work. As our clothes are restored to freshness, may we also daily restore and refresh our inner selves.

Blessing of a Den or a Study

Leader

Wisdom is radiant and unfading, and she is easily discerned by those who love her, and is found by those who seek her (Wis 6:12).

Residents

The human mind is a marvelous gift. May time spent in this room increase not only our knowledge and our intellectual pursuits but also enlarge and enhance our ability to be thoughtful and considerate human beings.

Blessing of the Living Room

Leader

"I was a stranger and you welcomed me. . . . Truly I tell you, just as you did it to one of the least of these who are members of my family, you did it to me" (Mt 25:35, 40).

out of the ordinary

Residents

Hospitable One, may we receive each person who enters this room as another Christ. May our guests experience your welcome. May our conversations and entertainment be a joy for all of us. May everyone feel at home here.

Blessing of the Family Room

Leader

How very good and pleasant it is when kindred live together in unity! (Ps 133:1).

Residents

Ever-loving Presence, may this room provide much relaxation and rest from the whirlwind of our full days. As we spend time here, renew and restore us. Let the joy of your heart fill us with true peace and contentment.

Blessing of the Bedroom

Leader

I will both lie down and sleep in peace;
for you alone, O [God], make me lie down in safety (Ps 4:8).

Residents

Abiding Presence, may all resting and sleeping here be a reflection of our resting in your arms. May you visit us in sleep through our dreams. As intimate times are shared here, may we remember the tenderness of your love.

Blessing of the Designated Prayer Room *(or prayer corner or chair)*

Leader

Whenever you pray, go into your room and shut the door and pray to your Father who is in secret; and your Father who sees in secret will reward you (Mt 6:6).

Other

Residents

Loving Presence, you woo us to your heart. You invite us to renew our relationship with you each day. May all who pray here be open to your mysterious ways. Keep calling to our hearts and reminding us of your abiding love.

Blessing of the Back Door

All extend hands toward the back door. After the psalm verse, the leader opens the back door.

Leader

[God] is your keeper; [God] will keep your going out
and your coming in from this time on and forever more (Ps 121:5, 8).

Residents

God of busy lives, we open this back door and remember that we will come and go often, from work, errands, social events, and many daily routines. As we come and go through this door, may we be mindful that everything we do is a part of our life with you. Grant us safety as we come and go.

Leader

Bless all spaces in this dwelling place.
May your love be evident in all the corners of this home.

All

Amen!

Optional suggestions:

A time of sharing stories about "home" could follow this blessing of the home.

What I remember most about my childhood home is. . . .

The home that I most enjoyed is . . . because. . . .

The first time that I left home. . . .

I want my home to be. . . .

The home that I think would be the most fun to live in is. . . .

We Remember the Bread of Life

The sections marked 1 and 2 could be read by alternate readers or prayed by the whole group in alternating sides.

All

Jesus, Divine Bread-Baker, each time we gather to break this bread we share its richness in the midst of our poverty, and we remember:

Leader

We remember who you are as the bread of our lives:

1. You are the One who enters into the hungry places of our hearts, wanting to convince us of your deep, abiding love.

2. You are the One who invites us constantly to choose life, even when our world, and sometimes our own inner places, tastes of death, pain, and weariness.

1. You are the One who becomes our spiritual energy, inviting us to yearn for truth and to grow from its treasures.

Leader

We remember how you gift us with this bread:

2. This bread is strength for us when times are tough.

1. This bread must be broken before it can be shared.

2. This bread, when taken within, transforms the quality of our presence.

1. This bread binds us together and tempts us to forgiveness and all the other particles which gather to form community.

2. This bread, which houses the sacred in common earthen gifts, proclaims that the ordinary is but a mask of the holy.

Leader

We remember what this bread asks of us:

1. To be patient with our own growth, to recognize the process of our journey, to yield to the nourishment which is waiting for us if we will but come to the table.

Other

2. To be your leaven so that faith can rise in the hearts of others.

1. To be so deeply wedded to compassion that our hearts always save a space for the tears of the world.

2. To give ourselves fully to the sojourning dimension of our lives, knowing that the manna of our God is blessing enough for our need as we yearn for our true home.

Leader

And finally, we remember:

All

That our hearts are filled with gratitude for this good gift.
Within us all that is holy cries out: Come, Bread of Life, come!

Evening Prayer

It is a valuable practice at night to spend a little while revisiting sanctuaries of your lived day. Each day is a secret story woven around the radiant heart of wonder. We let our days fall away like empty shells and miss all the treasures.

> —*Eternal Echoes,* John O'Donohue

Evening prayer is a time to re-enter peacefulness after the day's activities. We look back over the day to see how we were in relationship with the Holy One. We entrust ourselves to this Holy One as we prepare for sleep.

Recall the nearness of the Holy One. Envision yourself in the divine arms, held with care and with serenity. Pause for a few minutes of inner stillness and contentment. Continue with the following chant, or one of your own, or a favorite song.

Day Is Done *

Day is done, night has come,
I enter into peacefulness.
Now to sleep, now to sleep,
Wrapped within the arms of God.

Review of the Day

Gently look back over the day that you have just lived. Recall moments and situations which led you to gratitude, joy, hope, peace. Thank the Holy One for these moments.

Look again over the day you have just lived. Recall moments and situations which were difficult, stressful, disconcerting. Note any response of yours that you wish you could have changed. Bring your desire for change to the Holy One. Express your sorrow or concern. Once more place yourself in the loving care of the Holy One. Be at peace.

Other

Prayer for Peace and Protection Through the Night

*Pray or chant "Angels Before Me." * *

Angels Before Me

Angels before me, guide and direct me.
Angels behind me, guard and protect me.
Angels above me, keep watching over me.
Angels beside me, care for and comfort me.

Closing Prayer

Guardian of the Night, day is drawing to a close. I turn to you with all that my day has held and I entrust it into your care. All my joys and happiness, all my burdens and troubles, all that I am and all that I have, I now place into your hands. I trust that you will hold it for me 'til the morning light. May I enter into a restful sleep and rise with renewed energy in the new day. Thank you for being an abiding presence, a resting place, and a source of peace.

* See Appendix—Chants

Pentecost

A Prayer for Pentecost

Spirit! Power and Passion of my being,
press upon my heart your profound love.
Move through the fragments of my days;
enable me to sense your fiery Presence
consecrating my most insignificant moments.

Spirit! Source of Vision, Perceptive Guide,
permeate the moments of my choices
when falsehood and truth both call to me.
Turn me toward the way of goodness,
so that I will always lean toward your love.

Spirit! Blessing for the heart grown weary,
encircle me with your loving energy,
empower me with your active gentleness.
Deepen within me a faith in your dynamism
which strengthens the weak and the tired.

Spirit! Breath of Life, Touch of Mystery,
you are the ribbon of inner connection,
uniting me with the groaning of all creation.
Because of you, my life gathers into a oneness.
Keep me attentive to this interdependence.
Fill my being with a constant compassion
and a deep hope that knows no bounds.

Spirit! Dwelling Place, Sanctuary of Silence,
you are the home for which I deeply yearn.
You are the resting place for which I long.
I find both comfort and challenge in you.
Grant that I may keep my whole self open
to the transforming power of your indwelling,
that I may ever know the blessing
of your tremendous companionship.

—Joyce Rupp

The Fruits of the Spirit

The fruit of the Spirit is love, joy, peace, patience, kindness, generosity, faithfulness, gentleness, and self-control.

—Galatians 5:22-23

Surprising One, coming in ways I least expect, open me to your dynamic presence.

Awaken me, Surprising One!

Perceptive Guide, always available to direct my ways, advise me in self-discipline and decision-making.

Awaken me, Perceptive Guide!

Freedom Bringer, asking for my willingness to surrender, help me to let go, to let in, to let be.

Awaken me, Freedom Bringer!

Source of Power, providing stamina and strength for my soul, support me when I am weak and vulnerable.

Awaken me, Source of Power!

Arousing One, stirring up what is dead or stale, urge my stagnant, sleeping gifts into life.

Awaken me, Arousing One!

Divine Transformer, encouraging continued growth, grant me both patience and acceptance.

Awaken me, Divine Transformer!

Peacemaker, offering forgiveness and understanding, encourage me to communicate with love.

Awaken me, Peacemaker!

Bearer of Love, never-ending font of charity and compassion, may I share my goodness generously.

Awaken me, Bearer of Love!

Spirit!

Spirit! Nuzzling my life like a doe with her fawn,
protecting me from what could bring me harm,
nurturing me with the enriching milk of your love,
urging me to leap with inner freedom.

Spirit! As near to me as the mother robin
guarding her nest and warming her eggs,
readying me for the days of my flight,
telling me the plan is (always) for me to move out.

Spirit! I crave the closeness of your doe-care.
I love the warm assurance of the mother's nest.
I'd much rather stay safe, protected, nourished,
than be sprung free from security and fly away.

Ah, Spirit! But you tell me I cannot stay snuggled,
that my life is to bear your transforming power,
carry your love wherever I am, whatever I do,
no hanging onto the nest once I'm strong enough to go.

Was the Upper Room that way? A safe haven
until the whoosh of your wild wings
and the fire of your grace-filled breath
entered and empowered the disciples to go?
Are you telling me that the wild world is good,
that I will find you there, even as I bring you there?

Ah, Spirit! Draw me to the comfort of your breast,
nourish me with the power of your divine presence,
strengthen me with the courage of your love,
and then, shove me out of the nest when it is time.

—Joyce Rupp

out of the ordinary

The Spark of God

There are some persons whose great gift, in a dark age,
is simply to maintain a candlelight of humanity
and so to guarantee that darkness should not have
the final word.

—Robert Ellsberg

Spark of God, Spirit of Life!
I remember and celebrate your dwelling within me.

Divine Fire, you never waver in your faithful presence.
Amid the seasons of life, you are my inner illumination.

Ever-present Light, the spark of your inspiration has been
    with me
in every moment of my life, always available to lead and
    guide me.

Eternal Joy, the dancing flames of your joy are reflected
in my happiness and in the many ways that I delight in life.

Spirit of God, your fiery presence gives me passion
for what is vital and deserving of my enthusiasm.

Blazing Love, the radiant glow of your compassion fills me
with awareness, kindness, and understanding.

Purifying Flame, your refining fire transforms me
as I experience life's sorrow, pain, and discouragement.

Radiant Presence, your steady flame of unconditional love
kindles my faithful and enduring relationships.

Luminous One, you breathed love into me at my birthing
and your love will be with me as I breathe my last.
Thank you for being a shining Spark of Life within me.

—Joyce Rupp

Blessing for Pentecost

May the enthusiasm of Spirit leap incessantly within you and help you to live a vibrant life.

May the warmth of Spirit's fire be extended through your concern and care for all those who need your love.

May the blaze of Spirit's courage enable you to speak the truth and to stand up for respect, dignity, and justice.

May the undying embers of Spirit's faithfulness support you when you feel spiritually dry and empty.

May the strength of Spirit's love sustain your hope as you enter into the pain of our world.

May the clear light of Spirit's guidance be a source of effective discernment and decision-making for you.

May Spirit's patient endurance be yours while you wait for what is unknown to be revealed.

May the steady flame of Spirit's goodness within you convince you every day of the power of your presence with others.

May the joyful fire of Spirit dance within you and set happiness ablaze in your life.

May the spark of your relationship with Spirit catch afire in the hearts of those with whom you live and work.

May you be mindful of the Eternal Flame within you. May you rely on this Source of Love to be your constant ally and steady guide.

—Joyce Rupp

Astonished and Amazed

(See Acts 2:7)

like tulips long lying hidden
suddenly springing forth
making beauty out of sunlight

like soil caught and turned,
warm, moist, and ready for seed,
opening its heart for growing

like spring speaking to the day
about the goodness of the earth,
patterning green on every plain

like trickles of raindrops
smoothing earth's rough edges,
healing hardened hillsides

like all these quiet miracles
so is the coming of Spirit,
telling of the surge of life

urging me to gaze again
upon my very common days,
to look within and be amazed

—Joyce Rupp

Come, Holy Spirit

Open your mouth wide,
and I will fill it.

—Psalm 81:10

Come, Holy Spirit,

Help me to replace the busyness of my life with a simpler
lifestyle,
so I will focus on "the deeper things" in life and allow time
for others.

Nourish my yearning to understand and to appreciate
myself;
keep me from being too self-oriented and unmindful of
other's needs.

Fill me with trust in your consoling presence.
Calm me when I am anxious and troubled about many
things.

Help me to have the courage to empty myself of everything
that does not contribute to the transformation of this world.

Continue to create a deep hunger for you within me.
Feed me with "the finest wheat" of your joy, peace, and love.

Often replenish my weary spirit with an enthusiasm and
energy
that comes from surrendering my life to you.

Be my wisdom as I search for meaning in a world
fraught with pain, suffering, hostility, and division.

Keep me hungry for you, Source of Life,
so that I will always ache and yearn a bit for you.

—Joyce Rupp

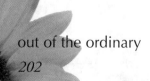

out of the ordinary

Thanksgiving

Gratitude for the Little Moments

Exhaust the little moment. Soon it dies.
And be it gash or gold, it will not come
Again in this identical disguise.

—Gwendolyn Brooks

gratitude, yes,
for all the big things
that stand tall,
thick with abundance,
joy, fruitfulness.
I cannot help
but applaud
their presence.

but deep thankfulness
for the bite-sized
pieces of my life?
I had not thought of them,
those little snippets of time
so easily consumed
in the hurry and blur
of pretentious days.

the little moments,
assumed and presumed,
slip quickly through
the fingers of my busy life.

November gestures
with a wrinkled brown hand,
beckons me wisely
to consider
those fleeting moments of grace,
in things quickly passing:

out of the ordinary

a walk on a musky-wooded path,
a cup of coffee silently savored,
a birdsong in the squeaky hours of dawn,
the gentle touch of a liver-spotted hand,
a loving letter from a grateful stranger,
a fading crescent moon in a royal blue sky.

I turn to gather
finely layered remnants like these
in the come and go of my days,
and discover, with surprise,
how quickly my inner room
is a harvest place of gold.

—Joyce Rupp

When

I must be thankful for what is
and stop thinking about what is not.

—Nancy Wood

In one of his journal notations Thomas Merton writes that we are always thinking that our life will truly be happy "when." We are not satisfied with what is currently our situation because we have it in our mind that our life won't be happy until something else occurs: when I have one more thing I want, when I get rid of that personality flaw of mine, when I can finally have life as I have always dreamed it to be, when I am truly successful, when I learn to pray better, when I find the right person in my life, when, when, when. . . .

Waiting for the "when" keeps me from appreciating what I now have. Longing for promises and dreaming dreams is not a harmful deed as long as the present moment is not overlooked, as long as gratitude rises for what is already here, as long as I do not base my happiness on what is still wanting. Thankfulness for what has already been given is the foundation for hoping for what is not yet.

Today I am going to put aside my "when this happens" and my "if only this could be" and my "when things get better" and my "as soon as I have this." I am going to harvest what I now have, gather all the many gifts that are already mine. I am going to observe what has been placed in the granary of my heart and marvel at the abundance.

I will stand before this heap of blessings and take a long, grateful look. I will say farewell to my "when" and be thankful for what is.

A Thanksgiving Blessing

May an abundance of gratitude burst forth
as you reflect upon what you have received.

May thanksgiving overflow in your heart,
and often be proclaimed in your prayer.

May you gather around the table of your heart
the ardent faithfulness, kindness, and goodness
of each person who is true to you.

May the harvest of your good actions
bring forth plentiful fruit each day.

May you discover a cache of hidden wisdom
among the people and events
that have brought you distress and sorrow.

May your basket of blessings surprise you
with its rich diversity of gifts
and its opportunities for growth.

May all that nourishes and resources your life
bring you daily satisfaction and renewed hope.

May you slow your hurried pace of life
so you can be aware of, and enjoy,
what you too easily take for granted.

May you always be open, willing,
and ready to share your blessings with others.

May you never forget the Generous One
who loves you lavishly and unconditionally.

—Joyce Rupp

Discover the Treasures

One August when I was in Alaska, I traveled to Hatcher Pass in the Talkeetna mountain range to visit the old Independence gold mine. There are many buildings at this historical site that are being restored so visitors can glimpse the miners' adventurous and challenging life. The following week I toured the Anchorage museum and looked at more photos and stories about the miners. As I walked through both places I was amazed at how tough their life was. Their rugged life demanded a tremendous endurance as they searched for the treasure of gold.

After I returned home from Alaska, I began thinking about how easy it is to gather certain treasures and how difficult it is to collect others. We can readily gather the things in our life that we enjoy: people, events, and situations that give us pleasure and satisfaction. For instance, it is natural to give thanks for "good health" but it's rare to hear someone give thanks for "bad health." Yet, there may well be a treasure in poor health if we look more closely. Perhaps such things as the kindness of others, certain insights about ourselves, or the strengthening of a relationship would not be known without the "bad health" situation.

There are some gifts we will only find when we dig deeply into our life, when we endure the hardship and the struggle as did the early gold miners of Alaska. Like some of the miners, it is possible that we will not find the treasures even though we go deep, far, and long in our search. But most of the time it is possible to glean something of value, some gift that helps us to grow or brings a return of meaning and joy to our life.

Recently I found myself whining and complaining about the continual packing and emptying of my suitcase, the irritation of airlines that either do not fly on time or never take off, the ceaseless stacks of mail, and the pressure of deadlines for writing assignments. Then I had the graced insight to see how I was focusing only on what I did not want in my life. I was failing to appreciate the blessing of each of those irritating things: my travel takes me to new people and allows me to invite them to spiritual growth; letters from both friends and

out of the ordinary

strangers alike often affirm my life or expand my compassion; being able to write is a gift I dearly value and I love to see how words come together in spite of the crunch of deadlines.

I thought of others who also need to ask if there is any gold beneath their problems or irritations. Do parents who give their all to children forget the treasure that these children are? Do older people struggling with the waning of their bodily and mental energies remember the jewel of their wisdom and faith? Do younger people who grow weary and worn out from work realize the gift of having a job and of being able to use their talents? Do those who struggle with depression or other illnesses notice the kindness and care of counselors, physicians, and other medical personnel?

As each of us gathers our treasures into our Thanksgiving baskets, let us not only find the obvious gifts but also look more deeply. Let us look in the struggles, the weariness, the toil, the heartaches, the frustrations and irritations, and mine the gold that lies hidden deep within each of them.

Memories of a Pilgrim Heart *

Do not forget the things your eyes have seen, nor let them slip from your heart all the days of your life.

—Deuteronomy 4:9 (JB)

Companioning God, grant me peace of mind and heart as I reflect on the past to see the ways you have been with me. May I look with a clear, inner eye and become aware of how you have both comforted and challenged me on my journey. I want to celebrate your companionship through the numerous twists and turns that have been mine. Speak to the pilgrim part of my heart. Encourage me to find the many, many aspects of my life that call me to gratitude and wonder. Remind me often that I am, indeed, a pilgrim on the way home to you. I need not be afraid of the wilderness and the moments of feeling lost, for you are always there as a loving Guide and Companion.

Look over your past year with "Exodus eyes," the eyes of a pilgrim, one who is always on the way. What do you find there amid the joys and sorrows? For what can you give thanks?

I remember:

. . . my Egypt situations of unfreedom that I have been able to leave behind,

. . . my burning bush moments when my faith was affirmed and my work renewed,

. . . my parting of the sea when I made it through difficulties and challenges,

. . . my companions who aided me in my wilderness times of doubt and confusion,

. . . my manna and quail that sustained my desert hunger and nourished me,

. . . my fire and cloud of other's steady fidelity that assured me of God's nearness,

out of the ordinary

. . . my hope in reaching the promised land of deeper peace, new-found joy, and a renewed sense of purpose.

After these remembrances, draw the path or road from your last Thanksgiving to this one. Mark significant places of challenge, opportunity, growth, joy, and consolation on your road (events, dreams, people, insights, intuitions, etc.). Reflect upon where you are now on this road. How has your Divine Companion been with you? Write a prayer of thanksgiving to this Divine Companion.

* See Exodus 3:1–6:13; 13:1–18:27; 40:34-37

Autumn Prayer of Acceptance

Autumn God, earth teaches me by her natural turning from one season to another. As she enters into the dying and rising cycle, she welcomes the changes. May I be open to the teachings in this season of autumn and turn, as autumn does, toward opportunities for my spiritual transformation.

When I accept only the beautiful and reject the tattered, torn parts of who I am, when I treat things that are falling apart as my enemies, walk me among the dying leaves. Let them tell me about their power to re-energize the earth's soil by their decomposition and decay.

When I fear the loss of my youthfulness and the reality of my aging, turn my face to the brilliant colors of October trees. Open my spirit to the mellow resonance of autumn sunsets. Brush your love past my heart with the beauty of golden leaves twirling from the autumn trees.

When I refuse to wait with the mystery of the unknown and when I struggle to control rather than to let life evolve, wrap me in the darkening days of November. Encourage me to enter into stillness and silent mystery, to wait patiently for clarity and wisdom.

When I grow tired of using my gifts to benefit others, take me to the autumned fields where earth freely yields the bounty of her summer. Let me become aware of how she allows her lands to be stripped clean so her fruitfulness will be a source of nourishment.

When I resist efforts to warm a relationship that has grown stale by my chilly indifference or resistance, let me feel the first hard freeze of autumn's breath and the death that this coldness brings to greening things.

When I neglect to care for myself and become totally absorbed in life's activities, let me see how animals gather sustenance and provide for their winter. Take me inside the caves of those who hibernate and remind me of my contemplative nature.

When I fight unwanted and unsought changes and when I seek to keep things just as they are, place me on the wings of birds flying

out of the ordinary

south for another season. Gather their spirit of freedom into my heart. Let me be willing to leave my well satisfied place of comfort for the discomfort of a long flight into the unknown.

Thank you, God of transformation, for all these lessons that the autumned earth teaches me.

Thanksgiving

cornstalks once tall and green
are now brown, dried, surrendered,
ears of corn with full kernels
shaped and turned golden
in a summer of sunshine and rain.
they fill to fullness wide wagons,
falling now into tall, round bins,
copious in their generosity,
abundant in unrestrained harvest.

this plenitude of the land
signals my own gathering of grain
as I turn to the bounty
found in the field of my heart.

all those daily gifts
that grace my humble path,
come tumbling forth,
like a corn harvest
of golden goodness.

they are my bin-full,
my thanksgiving treasure,
my wide wagon of richness.
they are my sureness
that the God of the harvest
still hurrahs.

—Joyce Rupp

Reflection on Autumn Days *

Response after each reflection: God of Autumn, your presence gives me hope.

A new season is moving in. We can sense its presence in the coolness of the breeze and the quick gusts of wind that wrap themselves around browning lawns and fading forest leaves. This time of transition belongs to more than just the earth. Inside of us there are also quiet changes sending us their signals to let go.

Trees of radiant green say goodbye to another year's growth. Their leaves break away, sailing to the ground. They tell us that in the deepest part of who we are, there is always a call to continue our transformation process.

Across the land truckloads of harvested fruits, vegetables, and grains make their way to market. Gardens and fields give of their gifts. Growers fill their baskets and wagons. Sometimes it is only when produce is gathered or grain is caught into wagons that the harvest is seen in its bounty. We, too, are meant to count our blessings even when the reaping at first looks sparse and lean.

Frost shakes the warmth out of autumn weather and shapes itself into the first hues of winter. We begrudgingly see the signs of future cold and emptiness, knowing full well that our hearts are not immune to this seasonal direction.

We wake up to misty mornings full of dampness, covered by clouds that hang low. Wetness rests on what remains of summer's beauty and fog tries to hide the road before us. We walk once more into the mystery part of life, recognizing that the inner journey also has its clouded, foggy pathways.

Color enriches autumn days with the last laughs of lovely marigolds and the visual flavors of rusted oaks and yellowed maples. A blessing called beauty kisses the sadness in their dying and makes of the ache a tender thing. When our own pain is great we look for beauty and know its soothing respite.

Geese are going south, as are all flocks of birds whose hearts lean toward the sun. They are in tune with the inside timing. We need that same gift of inner sensing so that we can be aware of our leaning toward the divine and follow what is being called forth in the depths of ourselves.

Beyond us, in distant places, there are other seasons of the earth and of the spirit. Wars with weapons are mixed with struggles of greed and power. Little children yearn to be fed and old people dream of days when there was peace enough for all.

Together

We are autumn people. We are always called to be in the process of growing and changing. May our minds and hearts be open to this inner season which is a part of us. May we trust you, Autumn God, who calls us to grow. May we find hope as we enter willingly into the dying that is needed for our transformation.

* See *Fresh Bread,* Joyce Rupp (Ave Maria Press, pp. 127–135) and *May I Have This Dance?,* Joyce Rupp (Ave Maria Press, pp. 129-140).

Transitions

Crossing Over

Crossing over
into the unknown,
crossing over
from a secure land
to one whose roads
I have never walked.

Companion and Guide,
you are my transition coach.

You say to me:
"Cross over the bridge.
Go ahead, come on over.
It's sturdy enough.

Don't look down, though,
or you might get terrified
and never walk across.

Don't look back too long
or you will lose courage
and want to stay
right where you are.

Hang on. Keep going.
That's what bridges are for,
to get you to the other side.
Trust me to protect you."

For all of us in transition
who have bridges to cross,
bless us, God of the journey,
gift us with the desire to go ahead.

Help us to trust
that the bridge will be strong
and the risk will be worth it.

—Joyce Rupp

A Prayer in Times of Transition

Guide of Weary Travelers,
take my hand as I wander
through the unnamed wilderness
in search of my true Home.

Companion of Those Who Journey,
assure me of your presence
while I search aimlessly
in the foggy land of "don't know."

Source of Wisdom and Guidance,
be the Star that leads me,
shine truth onto my path
and bless me with direction.

Wings of Shelter,
embrace me with your comfort
when the road is lonely
and life feels desolate.

Wellspring of Hope,
be my source of courage,
my fountain of faith
when I teeter toward despair.

Wind of Spiritual Liberation,
enter and unleash any shackles
that bind and restrict me
on the path of true freedom.

Heart of Compassion,
taste my tears,
heal my old wounds,
rest my pain in your love.

Bounteous Power,
dance in my bones,
sing in my spirit,
energize me toward action.

Endless Joy,
infuse my wilting spirit
with radiant vitality
and the sweet savoring of life.

—Joyce Rupp

Moving Into a Retirement Residence

"Abide in me,
as I abide in you."

—John 15:4

Loving Companion,

you know my thoughts and feelings as I make this significant move.

There is much I need to let go of and much I need to accept.

Comfort me when I am feeling the loss.

Encourage me to reach out to others especially when I feel all alone.

Lift my drooping spirit when I long to be living in some other place.

Enrich my life with new neighbors and acquaintances.

Erase negativism when it creeps into my conversations.

Draw cheerfulness out of me and help me to share this with others.

May your hope and kindness radiate through me.

Help me to accept my waning energy and my lessening independence.

Remind me of my treasures: good memories and the love of dear ones.

Grant me the grace to adapt to my new environment.

Let me see hidden sources of joy and happiness.

Draw me to your heart, O God, for you will never abandon me.

May I find peace and contentment resting in the arms of your love.

—Joyce Rupp

Prayer of Discernment

Spirit of Guidance, I see before me numerous choices and a decision to be made.

There is division in my heart. Sometimes I want none of what I find. Sometimes I want it all. Sometimes I want to give up making decisions and wish that the future would go away.

I entrust my decision-making into your hands, ready to do my part but also knowing that I cannot do this without your help.

Lead me through all the unsure, unclear, doubtful, hesitant, and questioning moments that are mine as I search to find the right way in which to go.

Grant me the grace to choose freely, without being attached to the outcome. I trust that you will be with me as I make my decision prayerfully and with faith.

Assure me that your peace will rest deep within me as I make the decision that seems best for me at this time. I may continue to experience feelings of turmoil and confusion, but deep within I know that I can return to that settled place in me where you always dwell.

Guide and Director of my life, I place my life in your hands. Lead me to the path that will best deepen and strengthen my relationship with you.

—Joyce Rupp

A Time of Difficult Transition

Divine Companion,
there's an ache in my heart
that stretches like a canyon,
crying out for all the familiar
faces and places of yesterday.

All the tears of my loneliness
gather themselves together quietly;
a hollow sadness rises in my soul
and presses against my every moment.

I am a lost one in a foreign land,
an orphaned one without a home.
I am out of place and unsettled,
yearning for peace that hides from me.

My feet take me through each day
but the rest of me just drags along,
wondering if I will ever feel at home,
doubting if this path is right for me.

Ever-Abiding Life Giver,
be a source of hope for me this day
as I adjust to this great change.
Be a sparkle of joy in my spirit
as I struggle with the pain of farewell.
Be a strong connector of love for me
as I leave many treasured ones behind.

Consoling One of My Heart,
assure me with glimmers of peace
that this transition can be a source of growth.
Grant me hopeful eyes to see beyond today
to the time when joy will tumble freely.
Lift up my heart and comfort me.

—Joyce Rupp

The Leaf

(A Meditation on Transitions)

You will need to find a leaf for this meditation. It is best to find a green leaf or one that is still alive. Be sure to show respect for all of life by asking permission of the leaf before you take it with you for meditation. Find a quiet place where you can be alone.

Find a leaf and hold it.

Notice everything about the leaf. Touch it and feel its texture.

Look at it closely, the edges, shape, size, color, veins, holes, or flaws.

Smell the leaf.

If you feel comfortable, take a tiny bite of the leaf and notice the taste.

Picture the leaf on a tree or bush or plant, fully alive, green, and growing.

Now, lay the leaf aside. Become still. Breathe deeply in and out a few times.

Let yourself become the leaf. See yourself on the tree, bush, or plant.

Notice your size, shape, etc.—all those things you noticed about the leaf.

Visualize yourself growing as the leaf:

You are in the quiet womb of the bud in the midst of winter, frozen, ice and snow.

Be with the quietness. . . .

You are in the stirrings of birth as spring pushes you out by the tree's energy and the pull of the warm sun. Be with this stirring. . . .

You are in your summer growth, stretching outward, larger, with more room for the sun's energy to penetrate and the rain to wash you. Be with this growth. . . .

You are now entering autumn, with less strength, cooler sun . . . finally the stem is too weak . . . you let go, twirl to the ground, lay there feeling dazed. Be with this dying. . . .

Let the rains of autumn come upon you. . . .

Slowly you fall apart, become gradually blended with the earth. . . . You become the rich humus. . . .

Now you feel a seed fall into your soil. . . . Surround the seed with your humus, your love. . . .

Feel the spring rain, stirring . . . notice a tiny shoot coming from the seed. . . .

See the shoot move up above the ground . . . with roots firmly planted in you. . . .

Now it becomes a bud, then an open, lovely flower. . . .

Enjoy the beauty of the flower that you have helped to birth. . . .

After this meditation time, reflect on which season of life you are in now—which leaf is most like your current life situation? Turn to the Holy One who journeys with you and give your heart in love and trust to this Holy One.

A Prayer for Those Who Journey

Response: Draw near, O God, draw near!

As we journey through life, we face fear of the unknown, doubts, hesitations, anxieties, and insecurities . . .

Life is an unfolding mystery, sometimes a painful search and sometimes a wonderful discovery. When our hearts are restless because they are pilgrim hearts whose Home is not here . . .

When our footsteps grow weary, when we stumble along the way, discouragement and doubt so easily come forth to greet us . . .

We are always learning what to leave behind and what to take with us as we move along the road of life. As we struggle to make good decisions . . .

We encounter you, God, continually in the constant cycle of setting out and coming home. Sometimes we allow life to be so busy as we travel that we miss your presence. When we need to slow our hectic pace . . .

Expectancy, anticipation, and courage rise up in our beings when we are open to your ways, God of the wilderness. As we search for reasons to hope . . .

In our journeying, we need a strong conviction about the beauty and goodness of life, a vision of hope that endures the pain and struggle, and a thread of love that weaves through all of our dreams. When we try to hold on to what gives our life meaning and purpose . . .

God Is With Us on the Road

Response: Help us to trust in you, God of the journey.

When we recognize our Egypts for what they are—addictions or unhealthy attachments, old sins that never seem to lose their grasp on us, ideas and actions that keep us in the dark, unloving decisions which bind us to the hard stones of our unforgiving hearts . . .

When we experience our dark moments of grief, pain, illness, failure; as we await the Angel of God to pass over the home of our selves, drawing us to hope and to new energy of life . . .

When we come to the Sea of Reeds in our lives and it seems as though our fears and anxieties will overtake us . . .

When we struggle to move on toward greater growth but find it difficult to let go of the past . . .

When we travel through those wilderness places of our lives where we feel lost, insecure, lonely, frustrated, discouraged, or overcome by busyness . . .

As we seek to find our way to truth, to wholeness, to better loving of others . . .

When we catch glimpses of the tremendous love you have for us and experience a deep, loving connection with others . . .

As we feel hope, joy, happiness rise in our hearts . . .

Together

God of the journey, we need a burning bush to set our hearts aflame with deep love of you. When the road of life seems long and tedious, when the dying and rising gets to be too much sometimes, be that pillar of fire by night and comforting cloud by day so that we can not only see the way but can be confident of your gracious presence which is our strength and our hope. We are on our way Home. Thank you for your nearness to us and for encouraging us to trust in you.

Delight of my Heart,
your joy echoes in my life.
I relish this happy transition
now shaping my days.

With the welcoming path before me,
I receive the promise of a new vista,
the benediction of an open road,
the pledge of an unfolding adventure.

Breath of Freshness,
my spirit expands and revives.
I taste the air of happiness
and breathe in welcomed newness.

You stir up hope-filled dreams,
restore my belief in all that is good.
You draw me toward contentment
and open the door to deeper trust.

How blessed is this passage of time
when confidence pervades my spirit
and peace permeates my mind.
I move forward with assurance.

Liberating Spirit,
soaring with freedom in my soul,
I fly with the gift of newfound hope,
my inner wings stretching wide.

Faithful Companion,
carry me in your abiding love.
Thank you for leading me closer
to that which encourages my growth.

Source of Joy,
you give me the gift of gladness.
Thank you for this blessed transition
and the chance to enter life more fully.

—Joyce Rupp

out of the ordinary

Valentine's Day

Containers of Divine Love

God of affection, devotion, passion, tenderness, and all forms of love, this day we thank you for the myriad ways that we have been given a touch of your goodness. We thank you for your many beneficent gestures:

. . . love that draws us to friendship and fidelity,

. . . love that leads us to kindness and compassion,

. . . love that stirs in our flesh and dances in our bones,

. . . love that lures us toward the sacred and serene,

. . . . love that calls us to new vision and growth,

. . . love that soothes our heartaches and gentles our pain,

. . . love that sees worth in each human being,

. . . love that believes in us and whispers with hope,

. . . love that sings in the seasons and sighs in the wind,

. . . love that taps on the door of forgiveness,

. . . love that longs for peace among all humankind,

. . . love that surprises and fills us with awe,

. . . love that sings praise for the face of earth's beauty,

. . . love that offers the hand of warm welcome,

. . . love that respects those who won't come too near,

. . . love that urges us to take risks and have courage,

. . . love that goes out to those from afar,

. . . love that embraces the shadow in us,

. . . love that sheds the old skin and welcomes the new,

. . . love that ripens our souls for the final journey home.

Source of Love, we offer thanks for how you are abiding in all of these forms of love. May the hearts we give and receive this Valentine's Day remind us of you, the One Great Heart, holding us all in the tenderness of your love.

out of the ordinary

Called to Love

For one human being to love another,
that is perhaps the most difficult of all our tasks,
the ultimate, the last test and proof.
The work for which all other work is but preparation.

—Rainer Maria Rilke

Jesus, you are "filled with love" for me just as you were for the rich young person who came to you. I, too, have riches, a wealth of love within me, that is meant to be shared. I yearn to have a deep desire for goodness so that I can leave some of the things I'm greedy for and focus my heart on the deeper values of your love. I yearn to love as you have loved (Mk 10:17-22).

Jesus, there are places within my heart that are still unfree and fearful. You made yourself available to the Samaritan woman and you pursued her with your strong belief in her inner treasures. Continue to pursue me and convince me of my inner treasures. I, too, am meant to be a person of love who announces hope to others (Jn 4:1-42).

Jesus, you told a powerful story of a person who stopped on a risky road to care for someone's wounds. Help me also to stop at the unpleasant places in my life, to be present to those who need a touch of love, especially on those days when my life is moving hurriedly and intensely. Grant me the courage to be less fearful of reaching out and walking with others who need a gesture of kindness and care (Lk 10:29-37).

Jesus, you welcomed a penitent woman who came to bathe your feet with her tears. You recognized the beauty of her love and the depth of her sorrow. There are tears within me which need to be shed for the pain I've caused and the hurt I've generated. You are a loving welcome for me as I come with my repentance. Thank you for all the times you've welcomed me home (Lk 7:36-50).

Jesus, you "loved your own, loved them to the end." You bent low before them, smelled their dirty feet, and washed them tenderly. You then asked them to share that same great love with others. I, your servant, am called to share my gifts and talents with those who are a part of my life. I am not meant to be a doormat for them but I *am* called to be generous and humble with the deeds I do. May it be so (Jn 13:1-15).

Jesus, you called your disciples friends. You recognized the great blessing they were for you on your journey. Thank you for the gift of my significant persons, for the privilege of walking through life with them. Remind me often of the strength and courage these loved ones give to me. May the joy I experience through them radiate love in my life to all who know me (Jn 15:1-17).

Praise to the Shaper of Hearts

Praise to the One whose love
stirs the ancient embers
sparks the breath of prayer

Praise to the One whose love
entices the wandering
beckons the confused

Praise to the One whose love
grows wings on the weary
dreams hope in the discouraged

Praise to the One whose love
dips deeply into diversity
pours forth boundless beauty

Praise to the One whose love
soothes with the ointment of mercy
transforms with the touch of compassion

Praise to the One whose love
threads the energy of friendship
stitches the strength of fidelity

Praise to the One whose love
tickles the soul with laughter
urges the heart toward joy

Praise to the One whose love
embraces the untamed
dances with the passionate

All praise to this Gracious One
All gratitude to this Beloved
All love to this Mentor of Friendship
All devotion to this Shaper of Hearts

—Joyce Rupp

Will You Be My Valentine?

"Peter, will you be my valentine?"
"Jesus, you know everything. You know I want to be your valentine" (rough translation of Jn 21:17).

Jesus also speaks to me:
"Will you be my valentine? Will you be my friend?"

Which is to say:

> Will you let me give you my unconditional love?
> Will you accept my peace for your tired and worn self?
> Will you receive my mercy and forgiveness?
> Will you believe in my love when everyone else has gone away or given up on you?
> Will you be generous enough to take my love to others when they need you?
> Will you be bread to my hungry, love to my needy, hope to my desolate?
> Will you love yourself well and believe in the gifts I've given to you?
> Will you trust me to always companion you?
> Will you lay down your life for me?

"Will you be my valentine? Will you be my friend?"

I listen to the invitation.
I look within and find "yes" answers
in my own February heart,
"Yes" because of dear friends
who have graced my days with love.

Their hearts are plainly flesh and earthen,
yet they touch me to your goodness.
Their hearts are weak and wounded,
yet they mend the torn in me.
Their hearts are tired and troubled,
yet they've time to give me rest.

My friends are loving pathways leading home,
home to where you are,
O Lover of All Hearts.

And so, I respond humbly, gratefully:
"You know everything.
You know I want to be your valentine."

—Joyce Rupp

A Heart Prayer

Reader

For surely I know the plans I have for you, says [God], plans for your welfare and not for harm, to give you a future with hope. Then when you call upon me and come and pray to me, I will hear you. When you search for me, you will find me; if you seek me with all your heart, I will let you find me . . . (Jer 29:11-14).

Response

Elusive One, I seek you with all my heart. The longing for you is planted deep within my heart. Hear my cry. Help me to discover you in all of life.

Reader

They are not afraid of evil tidings; their hearts are firm, secure in [God]. Their hearts are steady, they will not be afraid (Ps 112:7-8).

Response

I place my hope in your steadfast love, O God, believing that you are there in the most difficult of times. I praise and thank you for the gift of your compassionate love which encourages and strengthens me.

Reader

I have indeed received much joy and encouragement from your love, because the hearts of the saints have been refreshed through you . . . (Phlm 1:7).

Response

Thank you, God of love, for people who have come into my life and refreshed me. Thank you for all who have given me new hope on my journey, especially in my weary moments.

Reader

I will give them one heart, and put a new spirit within them; I will remove the heart of stone . . . and give them a heart of flesh (Ez 11:19).

Response

Forgive me, God, for those times when my heart was hard and unwilling to forgive or to offer understanding. Forgive me for my impatience with my own growth and that of others.

Reader

"Do not let your hearts be troubled. Believe in God, believe also in me" (Jn 14:1).

Response

Trustworthy One, when my heart is anxious, worried, or fearful, bring your calm and your serenity to me. Let my heart be filled with trust in your gracious care. Remind me often that I can come and rest in the dwelling place of your love.

Reader

So we do not lose heart. Even though our outer nature is wasting away, our inner nature is being renewed day by day (2 Cor 4:16).

Response

Transforming Presence, fill my heart with encouragement. Teach me that looks can be deceiving, that there may be a great mystery of spiritual growth in the events and situations that cause me discouragement and distress. Help me not to lose heart.

Reader

Faithful friends are a sturdy shelter; whoever finds one has found a treasure. Faithful friends are beyond price; no amount can balance their worth. Faithful friends are life-saving medicine . . . (Sir 6:14-16).

Response

Faithful Friend, thank you for the people who have been good medicine for my spirit. Their love has enriched my life and filled my heart with happiness. I am deeply grateful for their acceptance of me and their fidelity in giving me room to grow. Bless them this day with what they most need for their own spiritual path.

For Reflection

List several words or phrases that describe what your heart holds today.

List the things you most value about your friendships.

Which of the above scripture passages most speaks to your relationship with the Holy One?

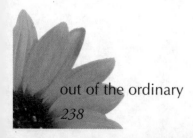

The Heart of Eternal Love

Heart of Love,
Source of all kindness,
Teacher of the ways of goodness,
you are hidden in the pockets of daily life,
waiting to be discovered.

Heart of Gladness,
Joy that sings in our souls,
the Dancer and the Dance,
you are Music radiating in our
cherished caches of consolation.

Heart of Compassion,
the Healing One weeping
for a world burdened and bent,
you are the heart we bring
to the wounded, worn and weary.

Heart of Comfort,
Sheltering Wings of Love,
Refuge for sad and lonely ones,
you embrace all who bear loss,
gathering their tears with care.

Heart of all Hearts,
the First and Best of all Companions,
you are the Gift secreted in our depths,
connecting us with others.

Heart of Understanding,
One who gazes upon the imperfect,
the incomplete, the flawed, the weak,
you never stop extending mercy.

Heart of Freedom,
the Uncontained Spirit bearing truth,
Great Liberator, forever calling to us,
you urge us toward unrestrained trust.

Heart of Generosity,
Abundance of insight and hope,
daily you offer us gifts of growth,
leading to continual transformation.

Heart of Deepest Peace,
Center of Tranquillity,
Resting Place at the core of our being,
you are waiting always for our return
to this sacred home.

—Joyce Rupp

Appendix—Chants

All of My Life

All of my life, all of my life, All of my life, I give to you.

All of the Stars

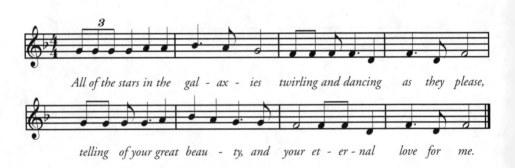

All of the stars in the gal - ax - ies twirling and dancing as they please,

telling of your great beau - ty, and your et - er - nal love for me.

Angels Before Me

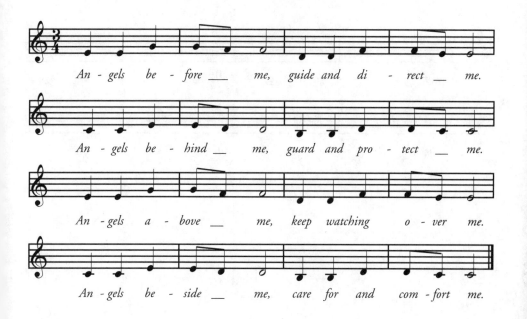

An - gels be - fore ___ me, guide and di - rect ___ me.

An - gels be - hind ___ me, guard and pro - tect ___ me.

An - gels a - bove ___ me, keep watching o - ver me.

An - gels be - side ___ me, care for and com - fort me.

Day Is Done

Day is done, night has come, I en - ter in - to peaceful - ness,

Now to sleep, now to sleep, wrapped within the arms of God.

Forgive

For - give, for - give, for - give, ___ for - give. Let my

heart be o - pen, for - give, ___ for - give.

Here I Am

Here I am. Here I am. Here I am. ___ Here I am. ___

Speak, for I am lis - tening. Speak, for I am lis - tening.

Speak, for I am lis - tening. I am lis - tening.

Holy One

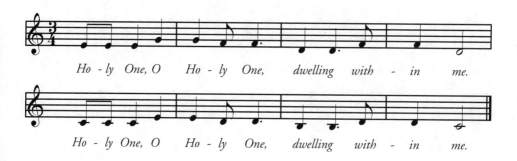

Ho - ly One, O Ho - ly One, dwelling with - in me.

Ho - ly One, O Ho - ly One, dwelling with - in me.

I Am Alive

I am a - live, I am a - live, I am a - live, a - live, a -

live. A - live, a - live, a - live. I am a - live.

Thank - you, Thank - you, I thank ____ you.

I Come As I Am

I come with my weak-ness. __ I come with my fail - ing. __ I

come with my strug - gle. __ I come as I am.

Light Our Way

Light our way, light our way, as we

jour - ney in the dark - ness.

Light our way, light our way,

gift us with hope for our world.

Mater Dolorosa

Ma _____ ter   Do - lo - ro - sa,

Mo - ther   of   Sor - row,   You   know ____   our   pain.

Moving On

We   are   mov - ing   on,   moving   on,   Yes,   the   time   is   moving

on.   So   go   with   courage,   go   with trust,   The   time   is   ripe   for

us.   The   time   is   ripe   for   us.

My Soul Rejoices

My soul re - joic - es in my God. My soul re - joi - ces in my God. ____ The God of jus - tice, The God of mer - cy, The God of com - pas - sion.

On a Journey

On a jour - ney, on a journey On a journey to the land of "don't know" On a journey, on a journey Take my hand now and guide me home.

Silently

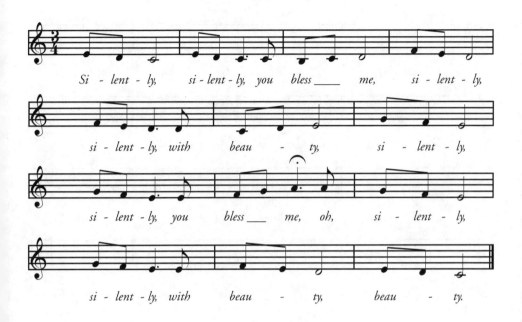

Si - lent - ly, si - lent - ly, you bless ___ me, si - lent - ly,

si - lent - ly, with beau - ty, si - lent - ly,

si - lent - ly, you bless ___ me, oh, si - lent - ly,

si - lent - ly, with beau - ty, beau - ty.

Spirit, Come

Spir - it, Spir - it, come in - to my life. ___

Spir - it, Spir - it, come in - to my life.

Fill me, Change me, Let me hear your voice. ___

Spir - it, Spir - it, come in - to my life.

Standing at the Door

Stand-ing at the door, Standing at the
door, Will you o-pen to me? Will you o-pen to
me? I will o-pen to you. I will o-pen to
you. Stand-ing at ___ the door, I will o-pen to you.

Thank You

Thank you for a night of rest.

Thank you for the morn-ing light.

Thank you for your pre-sence here.

Thank you for my life.

Those Who Brought Light

I re - mem - ber those who brought light. I re - mem - ber those
who brought love. I re - mem - ber those who brought God in - to my life. I will
go now and do the same. I will go now and do the same. I will
go now and do the same with my life.

We Have Seen

We have seen and we be - lieve. We have heard and we be -
lieve. We have touched and we be - lieve. We be - lieve.

Where Two or Three Are Gathered

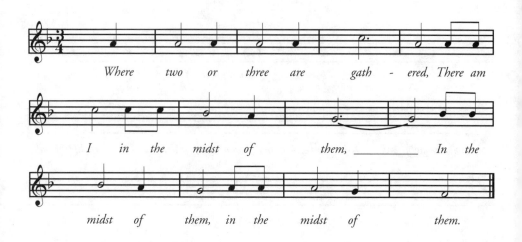

Where two or three are gath - ered, There am
I in the midst of them, _____ In the
midst of them, in the midst of them.

You Are With Me

You are with me al - ways, al - ways.
You are with me al - ways. _____

OUT OF THE ORDINARY: CHANTS . . .

Compact Disc   **Stereo Cassette**

*T*his companion recording contains prayerful Taize-like chants composed by Joyce Rupp and performed by Bridget Pasker, to enhance the many prayers and services in the book. The CD and Cassette provide a vocal rendering for all 23 chants found in the book's appendix. (54 minutes)

0-87793-936-5 / Stereo Cassette, $9.95
0-87793-937-3 / Compact Disc, $15.95

Out of the Ordinary: Chants, and additional copies of *Out of the Ordinary,* plus other books and audio cassettes by Joyce Rupp may be purchased at a local religious bookstore or from Ave Maria Press.

AmP ave maria press
Notre Dame, Indiana 46556-0428
P.O. Box 428
Phone: 1-800-282-1865, Ext. 1
Fax: 1-800-282-5681
E-mail: avemariapress.1@nd.edu